Mundi is a series conce... ...international essays and fiction.

Titles include:

A Passion for Ideas

Essays on the Scottish Enlightenment 2

A Passion for Ideas

Essays on the Scottish Enlightenment 2

George E. Davie D. Litt., FRSE

Edited by Murdo Macdonald

Polygon
EDINBURGH

© George Davie 1994

Polygon
22 George Square, Edinburgh

Set in Sabon
by Koinonia, Bury and
printed and bound in Great Britain
by Short Run Press Limited, Exeter

British Library Cataloguing in
    Publication Data
Davie, George E. (George Elder)
    A Passion for Ideas
    1. Scottish philosophy
    I. Title
    192

ISBN 0-7486-6147-6

The Publisher acknowledges subsidy
from the Scottish Arts Council towards
the publication of this volume.

Contents

Acknowledgements

'Hume, Reid and the Passion for Ideas' was first published in *Edinburgh in the Age of Reason* (Edinburgh University Press, 1967)

'Berkeley's Impact on Scottish Philosophers' was first published in *McGill Hume Studies*, edited by David Fate Norton, Nicholas Capaldi, and Wade L. Robison (Austin Hill Press, San Diego, 1979)

'Berkeley, Hume and the Central Problem of Scottish Philosophy' was first published in *Philosophy*, Vol 40, 1965.

'Victor Cousin and the Scottish Philosophers' was first published in English in *Edinburgh Review*, Issue 74, in 1986. A French version was published the previous year in *Victor Cousin: Les ideologues et les écossais*, by PENS, Paris.

'Edmund Husserl and "the as yet, in its most important respect, unrecognised greatness of Hume"' was first published in the *Hume Bicentenary Papers*, edited by George Morice, Edinburgh University Press.

'Husserl and Reinach on Hume's Treatise' was first published in *Speech Act and Sachervalt*, edited by Kevin Mulligan (Martinus Nijhoff, 1987)

Preface by Murdo Macdonald

In this second book of essays George Davie continues to explore the nature and influence of Scottish Enlightenment thought, not least by illuminating it with reference to its international roots and consequences. Davie explores here the influence in the eighteenth century of Irish thought in the person of George Berkeley; the central role in disseminating Scottish Enlightenment ideas played by the nineteenth-century French philosopher and politician, Victor Cousin; and the profound reappraisal of David Hume by Edmund Husserl, who pioneered phenomenology in Germany in the twentieth century.

At a time when it's easy to think that philosophy is going through a period outstanding only for its bland introversion, Davie's work – in which cultural and political questions are salient and in which history and ideas are seen as interdependent comes like a breath of fresh air. Davie is unequivocal in his view that philosophy is a cultural issue, it is not simply the preserve of a few experts. It is therefore no surprise to find him illuminating the dramatic interplay between philosophy and national identity in Scotland. He links the local and the international as a matter of course, for example: " ... we must always remember that what we are discussing is not a quarrel over professional standards in the philosophy departments of the West, but a cultural-political crisis with a dimension in international politics as to whether the Scots could keep alive in the nineteenth century the compromise, initiated by the Union, of identifying politically with the English, but of maintaining a distinctive national identity before the world ..." (from *Victor Cousin and the Scottish Philosophers*). In this interaction of local and international currents, Scottish philosophy is shown to be a formidable interlocutor in a continuing debate.

Since the publication of *The Democratic Intellect* in 1961, George Davie has been recognised as a key philosophical thinker and historian of ideas whose researches enable one not simply to understand the past, but also to give context to present developments. The value of his understanding of the Scottish generalist tradition in education is well established, but his explorations have also drawn attention to the civic power generated when, as a matter of course, the thinking of the expert is illuminated and complemented by that of the community.

Davie's advocacy of this democratic intellectualism, or critical generalism, is a crucial safeguard for an ever-more-inappropriately specialised world. It gives all Davie's work a particular cultural importance for the contemporary reader.

The value of the present selection of essays is enhanced by a perceptive introduction by Richard Gunn.

Adam Smith and Rousseau and *The Mirror Theory: Hume and Smith against Derrida* are printed here for the first time. The remaining essays have appeared elsewhere and thanks are due for permission to reproduce them.

Introduction

Suppose that, having been blind from birth, you suddenly gained your sight: could you predict that a cubic-looking object would not feel spherical, or a spherical-looking object cubic? How, in other words, would you set about interrelating your senses of sight and touch? Would not the question 'which was the sphere, which the cube' be, at least in the first instance, a question 'downright bantering and unintelligible' (Berkeley, *An Essay Towards a New Theory of Vision*, section CXXXV)?

Suppose that you were presented with a sphere of white marble: could you distinguish between its 'colour' and its shape or 'form' unless you were also presented with a sphere of black marble and a cube of white marble, so that you could see how it resembled the black sphere in one way and the white cube in another (Hume *A Treatise of Human Nature* Bk I, Part I, section VII)? Could even a person sighted from birth establish the distinction between shape and colour without tacitly making this sort of three-way comparison?

Questions of this kind, raised by Berkeley in 1709 and by Hume in 1739, introduce us directly to the minutiae of philosophies of perception. They are questions which have been of central importance to Scottish philosophy, from the eighteenth century onwards. In the present collection of essays George Davie, author of *The Democratic Intellect* (1961) and *The Crisis of the Democratic Intellect* (1986), explores the questions themselves, their origination – in, for example, the works of Berkeley – and their larger implications for European thought. Husserlian phenomenology, in particular, is demonstrated by Davie to have come into being through a critical and self-critical reception of Hume. In conventional histories of philosophy Hume's psychologism and Husserl's anti-psychologism are famous; Davie's achievement is to have drawn attention to the continuities which bridge this allegedly absolute divide.

Continuity, or rather the local and international conversation which allows apparently differing philosophical traditions to be interrelated, is a central concern of this volume. At the international level, the relation of Husserl to Hume is placed alongside Adam Smith's interest in questions he shares with Rousseau, and Derrida and Rorty make guest appearances as interlocutors in a still ongoing and, perhaps, Scottish-inspired debate. At a local level, Davie documents the role of Edinburgh's eighteenth-century Rankenian Club in establishing the reputation of Berkeley as a philosopher of perception to whom Scottish Enlightenment philosophy had to be able to respond. Scottish 'common sense' philosophy is in large part an attempt to meet the skeptical challenge which Berkeley's works were felt to contain.

Read as reconstructions of conversations, Davie's essays, however arcane and little-known their references and however historiographical their apparent sense, hurl thunderbolts against the prevalent modernist and post-modernist conception according to which philosophy amounts to the skeptical reflection upon itself of a single and solitary and monologically isolated soul. Conversation, *pace* Descartes who said (perhaps rhetorically) that he preferred to sit by his stove than to meet friends, just is the medium wherein philosophy can clarify itself, and expand. It is the atmosphere in which it can draw breath. Davie reports this when he says, in the essay on Victor Cousin (*infra*), that 'I can't be aware of matter or body as an object to myself, without also thinking of it as an object to other selves'. Conversational interaction with 'other selves' carries, with it, an epistemological charge; just as, conversely, only an epistemologically competent subject is able to sustain an interaction of a conversational sort. This sense of the importance of a to-and-fro interaction with others is central to the Scottish philosophical tradition so that, in his conversational reconstructions, Davie is carrying forward the programme of the commonsensical heroes – Hume, Smith, Reid and Ferrier – who map the territory which his own thought explores.

In what follows I attempt, briefly, to chart the outlines of the territory concerned. Such an attempt is risky, because Davie has always resisted the temptation to systematise what he powerfully argues is an ongoing and interactively developing body of thought. A systematisation can only be a snapshot recording a single moment in the development: it freezes diachrony into synchrony, threatening to turn a continuing 'passion for ideas' into a list of doctrines. However, the attempt is worth making because Davie, although famous as a historian of ideas, is much more than a historicist. The conversations he reports impinge on us, in so to say the first person, and so, as one move in the interactive self-reflection he commends to us, we need to take stock. Furthermore, conversation is not merely extensive but intensive. Philosophical discussion deepens into social theory (and *vice versa*) in the same movement as philosophers and non-philosophers – often the same people – play out differing roles. A conversational approach to philosophy tackles first- and higher-order – theoretical and metatheoretical, social and epistemological – points at the same time. The Adam Smith of the early but posthumously published 'History of Astronomy' and 'Of the External Senses' (both in his *Essays on Philosophical Subjects*, Glasgow edition), is equally the author of the passages in *The Wealth of Nations* (Vol II, p. 788: Glasgow edn.) which agonise over the epistemological competence of a subject conditioned by a social division of labour to play a public, or in other words a citizen-oriented, role. Scottish common sense philosophy proceeds in two registers, which are interconnected. The interconnection between the registers is the condition of the strength of each:

(i) There is a sort of republic of the senses, obtaining as between the senses themselves. For example, according to James Ferrier (his essays of the 1840s, republished in his posthumous *Lectures and Philosophical Remains* Vol II of 1866), we can integrate our senses of sight and touch only because we can touch our eyes (or, conversely, look at our hands). The republic of the senses is in this fashion interactive, as is any republic, and interaction and sensory integration go hand in hand. Before Ferrier, Smith (in his essay 'Of the External Senses') had made a similar point by means of the example of a hand touching a foot and, a hundred years after Ferrier, Merleau-Ponty in his *Phenomenology of Perception* supplies a beautiful illustration of Davie's thesis concerning ongoing and international conversation when he explores the complex sensory implications of a phenomenological experiment which proceeds as follows: grasp an object with one hand, eyes open, and then close your eyes and with your other hand grasp the grasping hand. The experiment is vertiginous, because the sensation of grasping the grasping hand threatens to turn the grasping hand into something very closely approximating to dead meat. What Smith and Ferrier and Merleau-Ponty in their different ways imply is that 'the theory of the body is already a theory of perception' (*Phenomenology of Perception* Part Two), and *vice versa*. Their common concern is with the circumstance that a theory of the interrelation or interaction of the senses is also, at the same time and 'in the same movement' (as Merleau-Ponty might have said), a theory of the interrelation and interaction which goes forward between our first-person and our third-person senses of our embodied selves. Sartre, in his famous chapter on 'the look' in *Being and Nothingness* (Part Three, ch I, section IV), declares for the same view although prioritising the sense of sight over and above the sense of touch which the Scots, more mundane and less Cartesian, thought might be able to do the integrating and totalising job.

One is for oneself both a first- and a third-person object. One's entire body is an organ of perception whilst at the same time being an object which can be felt and seen no less assuredly than can a beer glass or a football stadium or a chair. The integration or interrelation of our senses *just is* the integration of our first- and third-person self-understandings. We can see and feel ourselves in almost the very same manner as others can see and touch us. We can be objects for others in much the same way as, flipping over from first-person subjectivity into third-person objectivity, we can regard ourselves as sick or happy, as miserable or as triumphant. Self-reflection is the key, inasmuch as self-reflection is the shared condition of interrelating the senses, of mapping first- and third-person perceptions of oneself on to one another, and of gaining purchase on the interactive flow as between first- and higher-order (theoretical and metatheoretical) intersections in which every good conversation consists. Experience is more rich in insights – this was the point emphasised by Reid *et al* against Berkeley – than any *a priori* reconstruction of experience could ever be. Experience *is* interaction, and *vice versa*, because it can draw upon the resources of self-reflection. There is a sort of 'dialectic of experience' (Hegel *Phenomenology of Spirit* Intro.), which relates ourselves to our world or worlds. Reflective judgement (Kant in his *Critique of Judgement* and Kant on the productive imagination in the *Critique of Pure Reason*) assumes priority over determinate judgement because whereas determinate judgements bring particulars beneath known universals the condition of reflective judgement is that it generates universals out of (self-)reflection upon the particulars themselves. This is less a matter of inductivism – a sheer, empty and monological abstraction of a genus from a species – than a celebration of what can be achieved by *sensus communis* or, in other words, commonsense. A reflective judgement (Kant) or a perceptual judgement (the Scots) abut on to a common world. We can not just hear and see but interactively reflect upon and talk about the same thing. The republic of the senses entails (and *vice versa*) a political republic which relates selves to others. This means that

(ii) there are social conditions of self-reflection: *pace* Descartes, monologically warming a stove amounts to nothing resembling an epistemologically privileged viewpoint. Epistemology is bound up with social practice. The notion of common sense as *sensus communis* (public or shared sense) both underpins and is constituted by our 'endeavouring' to view our judgements 'with the eyes of other people, or as other people are likely to view them' (Smith *The Theory of Moral Sentiments* Part III, ch 1). What Hume (loc. cit.) calls 'distinctions of reason' – as between the white and the black cube and the black and the white sphere – can amount to more than the sort of inductivism which Karl Popper is famous for challenging only because we can see ourselves as others see us. Epistemologically, one can get by (only) with a little help from ones friends. Knowledge is public rather than private. Self-consciousness 'exists only in being recognised' (Hegel *Phenomenology of Spirit* para. 178; cf Davie *The Crisis of the Democratic Intellect* Part III, chs 10–11). A public or social crisis is, thus, an epistemological crisis and *vice versa*. Descartes retreated to his stove in the course of horrendous wars, and the epistemologically-oriented Scots were wrestling with the problem of reconstituting what had been a small nation.

This makes clear what should be the answer to those – and they are legion – who declare that Scottish philosophy's concern with detailed points of perception amounts only to narcissism or introversion. Why talk about phenomonology and an intersection of the senses – why problematise *common* sense – when one's political community is falling apart? The Scottish and

Davie-oriented answer would be to the effect that epistemological and social crises are one and the same. Just as philosophy devolves into politics, politics devolves into epistemology. A glory, both local and international, springs from the same set of points.

Nietzsche (*Daybreak*, para 117) reports that 'We sit within our net, we spiders, and ... whatever we may catch in it, we can catch nothing at all except what allows itself to be caught in precisely our net'. This is the most famous recipe for post-modernist solitude and relativism; Davie calls this back into an intersubjectivity which develops upon, and summons, a common world. Relativism fails, because sensory perceptions dovetail upon a world whereof we can speak. Epistemology, *à la* Descartes, fails because it has no sense of a common world. Read Davie, in and through the local and international and solitary and intersubjective and epistemological and political points he reports, and never see the land we call Scotland or the North British peninsula, in the same way, ever again.

Richard Gunn
Edinburgh

Hume, Reid, and the Passion for Ideas

Let me begin with a pertinent question. This Scottish Enlightenment – was it an exotic bloom where Scotland was concerned? How far was it the mere preserve of a leisure class, which had immured itself in the New Town of Edinburgh? This point of view, though still widespread, is, I believe, seriously confused, being due to a failure to distinguish the aesthetic side of the Scottish Enlightenment, as discussed by Professor Youngson, from the side I wish to discuss: the passion for ideas. The artistic subtleties of the townscape of the New Town – the Claude-Poussin effects, for example, – may well have been exotics from a Scottish point of view, but this remoteness from the nation was not so true of the intellectual life. The ideas argued over at the dinner tables of Charlotte Square, though they might derive ultimately from the Universities of Germany or the Salons of Paris, were eagerly overheard and assimilated throughout Scotland, and freely commented on and criticized by persons of the most varied backgrounds.

This nation-wide concern with ideas was a remarkable state of affairs, and one which was perhaps responsible for the Scottish Enlightenment's intellectual seriousness. Elsewhere enamoured of abstractions and oversimplifications, the philosophy of *les lumières* was able to impinge on Calvinist Scotland only by dint of redrafting its whole intellectual programme in a realistic version which would do justice to the complexities of the human situation. Welcoming the Enlightenment demand for radical transformation of the conditions of social life, the Scots at this time flatly rejected the simplifying philosophy of reductive empiricism which was everywhere the accepted vehicle of forward-looking policy; in its place, they developed a historically-minded realism, which, durable and profound, avoided the characteristic limitations of the eighteenth-century outlook.

This markedly individual, not to say exceptional, character of the Enlightenment in Scotland – for long overlooked in the English-speaking world – has been duly noted on the Continent. Following up a line started by Charles de Rémusat's classic study of *la philosophie écossaise*, Paul Hazard has pointed out that the Scots had no sooner made their debut in the intellectual movement of the eighteenth century, than they decisively overthrew and outdated its basic principles, imposing a new direction. Already by 1730, Francis Hutcheson, father of the Scottish Enlightenment, was critical of Lockeian empiricism, which everywhere else in Europe was beginning to be the recognized standard. Taking up where Hutcheson left off, David Hume, in his *Treatise of Human Nature*, 1739, shattered beyond repair the whole basis of the principle of Enlightened rationality. Responding to his challenge, Thomas Reid and Adam Smith quickly carried through a radical reconstruction – in 1764 and 1775 respectively – which left the eighteenth century behind it: the first preparing the way for the *classe de Philosophie* era, and even for modern French Phenomenology, the second lucidly pointing forwards to the industrial society with its problem of 'alienation' and atomization. Elsewhere the *siècle des lumières* was confidently brilliant; in Scotland, the modern world had already begun.

Taking for granted, as the distinguishing quality of the Scottish Enlightenment, this ability to look beyond eighteenth-century limits, I want to raise the question of the peculiarly national experience which at once stimulated Scottish far-sightedness and kept it looking in fruitful directions. In order to get light on this matter, it is, I believe, essential to bear in mind a circumstance which is too often forgotten – that the impact of the European Enlightenment on Scotland coincided precisely with the difficult post-Union decades, when Scotland was struggling to adapt, to the exigencies of the new political partnership with England, a native inheritance of institutions which had been conceived on Continental lines, partly through the Franco-Scottish connection, partly through contacts with the Netherlands. It was, one might say, this practical experience of adapting un-English institutions to the Union that made the Scots so very reserved in their recognition of the glowing promise of the Enlightenment. In this way, *la crise de conscience Européenne* (as Paul Hazard called it), the all-out intellectual revolt against the Baroque legacy of the seventeenth century, was limited and modified in its impact on Scotland by the counter-experience of a sort of *crisis of national existence*, in which the threat or reality of assimilation to England brought home, to the Scots, the value of their native inheritance of institutions, legal, ecclesiastical, educational.

In order to show how the Scottish Enlightenment fused national with intellectual aims, let us take

3

Francis Hutcheson's neglected but important pamphlet of 1735 – *An Address to the Gentlemen of Scotland*. A sort of manifesto of the Scottish Enlightenment, this remarkable document takes as its starting-point the spirit crisis, which, brought on by the Union, was in process of disrupting the established pattern of Scottish polity. The specific question at issue, as Hutcheson posed it in his pamphlet, was whether, under the London-centred incorporation of the two countries, the English arrangement of subordinating the Church to the State might not undermine the very different Scottish system which, modelled upon Continental example – not just Calvin's Geneva, but also the Dutch reform, as well as French protestantism in its legalized period – involved a delicately maintained balance between the democratic rights of the people and the authority of the state. The danger of Scottish assimilation to England in this spiritual sphere was, Hutcheson felt, not a merely theoretical one. A decree of the London Parliament, carried through in defiance of the Act of Union, had put effective control of Scottish ecclesiastical patronage in the hands of the crown, not only depriving Scottish congregations of their established right in the matter of appointing ministers, but in addition nullifying the influence of the Scottish gentry. More and more a situation had developed, Hutcheson thought, in which Scottish pulpits would be filled, not by well-educated Presbyterian pastors who would give a hand to the cause of the country's improvement, but by new Government placemen, whose overriding aim was simply to keep things quiet, thereby inducing the Church of Scotland to forget its progressive heritage as a leading part of the

4

Calvinist-Presbyterian internationale, and to turn itself into pale imitations of the conformist and erastian Church of England.

The *never-to-be-forgotten Hutcheson*, as his admiring pupil, Adam Smith, was to call him, succeeded in establishing the credit of the Enlightenment with the sober-minded Scots, only because he was able, in declarations like the one under review, to present the illuminist principles in such a way that they seemed the sole viable answer to the post-Union spiritual crisis. Appealing to the national spirit of the Scots, dormant since the Union, Hutcheson outlined a programme for the moral and material advancement of Scotland. Refusing to allow the anti-Union platform of the Jacobites a monopoly of Scottish nationalism, Hutcheson called for a liberal-minded patriotism which would operate within the framework of the Union. The lairds and smaller gentry, instead of, as heretofore, shirking their public responsibilities, must put themselves forward as the defenders and promoters of the cause of the nation. The first necessity, he emphasized, was to check the Anglicizing assimilation which, set in motion by the crown authorities, was sapping the spirit of the people. But at the same time, it was also necessary for the lairds to hold the nation together, in the face of the opposite danger of one of these retreats into sour-faced individualism, to which the Calvinist-minded democracy of Scotland was always excessively prone. If Scotland was to be a *progressive* nation, and not a backward one – and this Enlightenment principle was foremost in Hutcheson's mind – it was necessary that the spiritual leadership of the country should belong neither to Government-paid nominees intent on the *status quo*, nor to wild-eyed enthusiasts, eager to bring back the anarchy of Covenanting times.

How was this policy of patriotism within the Union going to attack the problem of Scottish backwardness? According to Hutcheson, the key to the situation lay in the proper employment of Scotland's native institutions – especially the Universities which, recently reorganized on the Netherlands model, constituted her chief national asset. The main thing to be watched here, Hutcheson argued, was that the democratic policy of the open door, valuable in itself, should not be allowed to conflict with the aim of improving the intellectual standards of the Universities. What the Universities must aim at was the production of ministers with sufficient culture and general education to enable them to co-operate with the lairds in promoting the cause of general progress. In this way, Hutcheson's policy for a national-minded, liberal-minded Enlightenment provided a background to the ethics of public spiritedness which was to be the centrepiece of his Moral Philosophy.

The idea of a limited nationalism which Hutcheson put forward as the platform of a Scottish Enlightenment, was, however, at best, premature; and the compromises he called for began to break down in the tense years which led up to 1745. But this time completely out of patience with the Union, a considerable section of the Scottish nation was preparing to re-establish parliamentary independence by force of arms, restoring the Stuart dynasty and reviving the Franco-Scottish alliance. In this decade of plots and counter-manoeuvres, young Scotsmen of talent, instead of rallying to Francis Hutcheson's appeal for unity in the name of nationalism of the spirit, were preparing to take opposite sides in an imminent civil war; and the rising of '45 saw the economist-to-be, Sir James Steuart, busy at Holyroodhouse as Prince Charles' adviser, while the future philosophical historians, Adam Ferguson and William Robertson, rallied to the Government side in defence of the Union.

It was during this critical decade, when Scotland found herself faced with the unendurable alternatives of continuing the English Union (with all its humiliations) or of resuming the French alliance (with all its dangers) that the challenging genius of David Hume suddenly emerged, to generalize his country's experience of inextricable dilemma, into a profound critique of the basic Enlightenment principle of intellectual optimism. His studies at la Flêche, his business experience at Bristol, had already acquainted him, at first hand, with the divergence between the extroverted Baconian spirit of the English and the inward-looking Cartesianism found across the Channel. Inspired by this experience to anticipate, indeed to improve upon, the Kantian insight that this contrast between Continental rationalism and English empiricism constituted a fundamental cleavage in the human point of view, David Hume summed up the situation in that remarkable concluding chapter to the *Treatise*, Book One, by opposing to one another, a pragmatic attitude recognized as typically English, and an intellectualist attitude associated with France and the Continent, as at once complementary to one another and yet mutually irreconcilable. The essence of human intelligence, he says, consists in the precarious and perhaps impossible balancing-act, of alternating between two rival, incompatible positions – on the one hand a Cartesian intellect which will be satisfied with nothing but clear and distinct ideas, and which seeks ultimate system; on the other hand, an Anglo-Saxon pragmatism which has no time for theory, and instinctively knows not to press the argument too far. Confronting the apostles of the Enlightenment with these irreconcilabilities and antinomies whose existence they had so jauntily ignored, David Hume – here too forestalling Immanuel Kant – bade them rethink their intellectual foundations. Until they faced up to this ultimate contradiction between the intellectual factor and the pragmatic, their optimism of civilization was based on the blindness of bad faith.

Preoccupied with undermining the Enlightenment in its global setting, Hume's philosophy was, nevertheless, especially destructive of the particular version which Hutcheson was trying to put over in Scotland. From Hume's point of view, the pair of contrasting positions which Hutcheson, intent on a media via, had condemned as extravagant extremes – on the one hand, the intellectual indifferentism of pragmatic-minded Anglican conformists, and, on the other hand, the soaring, insatiable quest for metaphysical clarity à la Descartes, which Scottish Calvinists, following their Continental brethren, regarded as the prerequisite of the leap of faith – were, each in their different ways, far more defensible and far more profound than the all-reconciling middle way which Hutchesonians recommended as the alternative to either. Confronted with clerical critics from the anti-Calvinist, Hutchesonian camp, Hume retorted by avowing his intellectual solidarity with the seventeenth-century French divines whom orthodox Scottish Calvinists admired – men like Huet, Bishop of Avranches, who approached religion by way of the metaphysical intellectualism of unsatisfied Cartesian self-doubt. Then, having thus administered this first shock to the Scottish Enlightenment by identifying with a position it regarded as a morbid scepticism, Hume went on to deal an even deadlier blow to its pride of intellect. Agreeing that the Continental ideal of the pursuit of absolute clarity, however well-founded, and as he believed, justifiable, nevertheless in the last analysis led to the most intolerable scepticism, he pointed out to the apostles of Enlightenment that the proper answer to the sceptical regress wasn't the apparatus of self-conscious intellectuality of which Scottish educationalists were so fond, but the deliberately unintellectual attitude of the pragmatic Englishman. The Enlightenment had, Hume went on, gone astray in picking the would-be philosophical Francis Bacon as the Englishman most worthy of admiration. On the contrary, the sort of Englishman Europe should honour was the one it least appreciated – the unreflective country gentleman of the type of Addison's Sir Roger de Coverley, who had no interest whatsoever in philosophical first principles.

Passing from metaphysics to ethics and economics, Hume's genius, with a final characteristic flourish, completed the discomfiture of Enlightenment optimism, by a sort of Manichaean interpretation of human history, which sees it as a battle-ground between much the same pair of contrasting and sometimes complementary principles as we have already encoun-

9

tered in his metaphysics – the one down-to-earth and pragmatic, the other a counter-principle of an intellectual nature which aspires to a sort of metaphysical order and unity. The materialist conception of history, with its reductive, economic explanations, is, Hume allows, fruitful and satisfactory in regard to those institutions where the pragmatic principle is uppermost. However, there is, at the same time, always the limiting factor (too much overlooked by sociologists and economists) that the operation of the pragmatic principle of Enlightened self-interest tends to be cut across by the metaphysical counter-principle which, fastening on to and exploiting the religious side of experience, inspires various fanaticisms.

Applying this point of view to the social experience in which he was crucially caught up – the Scottish post-Union experience – Hume proceeded to formulate a view of the problem of Anglo-Scottish symbiosis which contradicts every principle put forward by Hutcheson. Putting himself first at the pragmatic point of view, Hume argues that there is no difficulty in principle as to how backward Scotland is to catch up with her richer neighbour. Given sufficient time and scope, *free trade*, by its automatic operation, would achieve the miracle. There is, therefore, no need of an organized national effort to reawaken the Scottish public-spiritedness, such as Hutcheson postulated. On the other hand, Hume is perfectly aware that this pragmatic point of view is only a partial one. Correcting it by bringing into view the metaphysical aspirations of man, we must bear in mind how the dark fanaticisms of the Scots could interfere with the beneficial automatisms of free trade. Difficulties of this kind might, no doubt, seem to warrant some state-interventionism, but, in any case, the appropriate kind of remedy here (if indeed any remedy is possible) would, Hume thinks, be found not so much in the kind of scheme Hutcheson favoured – encouragement, by the state, of liberal education – but, in the very arrangement Hutcheson most abhorred: a state-subsidized clergy, somewhat on the Anglican plan. A comfortable, pragmatic parson, who knows on which side his bread is buttered would, Hume thinks, provide a far more promising check on Scottish fanaticism than a restlessly meddlesome clergy who pride themselves on their general education and liberal view.

Overlooked by the rest of Europe, the force of Hume's philosophy was first felt at home. An affront to everything the Scottish Enlightenment stood for, the Humian scepticism had aroused instant opposition among progressive-minded Scots of the Hutcheson type, who henceforth made it their chief intellectual aim to face up to this disconcerting blend of the most outrageous provocation and the most genuine profundity. To begin with, adequate answers to the *Treatise* were hard to come by, but, in the fifties, Lord Kames made a first break-through; and, with the advent of Adam Smith and Thomas Reid, the Scots not only managed to regain their shaken intellectual confidence, but were able to alert the Continental countries to the weaknesses in the Enlightenment system which had been uncovered through Hume's criticisms. In this sense, the European reaction against the excesses of eighteenth-century illuminism not only started in Scotland, but found in *la philosophie écossaise* some of its sanest and most influential exponents.

If we are to do justice to the long-continued Continental impact of the Scottish sequelae to Hume, if we are to appreciate why, even in the nineteenth century, a man of Théodore Jouffroy's stature could insist that *l'Ecole d'Edimbourg* had a central, not a merely exotic, interest to Europe, it is essential always to bear in mind that the historical background not merely to Hume's writings but to those of his chief Scottish critics – *le bon Thomas Reid* and the sagacious Dr Smith – was a Scotland which had been reinvolved in Europe as the result of the '45, and which had been reminded by the rising of the foregone and almost forgotten possibility of disconnecting itself from England, and renewing its Continental ties. From the European point of view, perhaps the most interesting and original feature of Scottish Philosophy was this – that the experience of revolt had made the Scots acutely aware of the profound intellectual cleavage, so shocking to Enlightenment optimism, between the values the English stood for, and those upheld by the Continentals. Found even in writers who were passionately concerned to reassert and realize the Union, like Adam Ferguson and Principal Robertson, this abstract Scottish critique of English insularity, this generalized view of the Union as, in some sense, a betrayal of Europe, gets its clearest expression from those writers who took the other side and endured exile in consequence. What Hegel and Marx, therefore, would find to interest them in the writings of the Scottish Jacobite leader, Sir James Steuart, whom they both admired so much, wasn't just a system of economics different from Adam Smith's, but an outspoken preference for the Continental principle of a conscious inwardness, preoccupied with the intellectual ideal of *system*, as against the contrasting English values of piecemeal, pragmatic procedures which are uninterested in anything but externals.

Adam Smith was, in his own way, as deeply involved as his fellow-economist, Sir James Steuart, in this critique of English insularity, and makes it the central theme of one of the most important and original sections of *The Wealth of Nations*. Taking up David Hume's economic question as to whether backward Scotland, under the free-trade conditions provided by the Union, could even catch up with the immense superiority of her predominant partner, Adam Smith pointed out that the question, posed in that form, attributes far too much advantage to England, and forgets certain counter-assets which Scotland and other countries like Scotland could count upon. Drawing upon his experiences, as a student, of being educated, partly under the exclusive system peculiar to England, and partly under the more open system which the Scots had developed after Continental Calvinist models, Adam Smith was able to see clearly (what few at the time discerned) that a scheme of state-supervised, compulsory, elementary education on lines pioneered by Scotland, and other Presbyterian countries, was very well suited to the coming era of industrialization and the factory-system, not only as a means of *technical* training but even as a specific against 'alienation'. By reason of this educational differentiation, Scotland had, thus, a very definite economic asset which England lacked; and the Scots, if they cultivated properly this advantage, might hold their own in the otherwise difficult free-trade relation with England. Taking a remarkably penetrating and far-sighted view of social-intellectual factors, Adam Smith thus answers Hume's problem about free trade.

But what of Hume's lurking fear that fanaticism of spirit might interfere with the beneficent long-term effects of free trade? Conceding that there was a certain danger of this, Adam Smith went on to reject Hume's suggestion that a state subsidy to the clergy was the proper way to check public fanaticism. In the modern world, Smith argues, community-leadership wasn't a monopoly of the ministers of religion, but was the accepted responsibility of the professional classes generally. If the state was to discourage the narrowness of fanatical views, its aim should be not the out-of-date and, in any case, ineffective remedy of a subsidy to pastors and priests, but an official injunction (to be ratified by state supervision) that the professional classes get not blinkered and merely specialized training, such as is all they received in England, but also general courses in science and philosophy such as might encourage a balanced view of the human situation. Having begun by recommending, to the world public, elementary education more or less on the Scottish model, Adam Smith rounds off this system of a pedagogy for a modern, industrialized society by a generalization based on the social function of universities in Scotland.

This shift of emphasis from the clergy to the laity, and from religious and confessional instruction to general public education, was the capital contribution whereby Adam Smith, improving on his admired master, Francis Hutcheson, was able to turn the tables on Hume's sceptical pessimism, and point towards a scheme of Enlightenment more viable than that of the eighteenth century. What Adam Smith had done was reformulate Hutcheson's scheme of patriotism within the Union so as to give Scottish education pride of place over religion. But at the same time, in this doctrine of the relation of education and industry, Adam Smith, with his generalizing power, had more than Scotland in mind, and was giving the lead to a revolution which, carried through in nineteenth-century Europe, was to make Professors and school-masters, rather than priests and ministers, the responsible sources of public illumination.

Consequent on the insights of Adam Smith, the Scots, always education-minded, began to take very seriously the Continental affinities of their pedagogical system, confidently preferring it to the insularity of English arrangements. Whereas David Hume, with an eye to social advantages within the Union system, was in favour of sending Scottish boys of good family to English Eton, other representative Scots (of comparable standing) considered that the cultural advantages of education in the Scoto-Continental style was something of supreme importance. Thus, Hume's friend, the Baron Mure, disapproving of the narrowly classic bias of English education, imported a tutor from France, who would give the boys a general and philosophical grounding in the Continental style. For social reasons, indeed, the boys had to be sent to Oxford for a term or two, but the Baron counteracted its effects by putting them to Paris for an equal period as well as by arranging that their studies, in the one and in the other place, were to be supervised by a Francophile Scottish philosopher, George Jardine, later to be celebrated as the colleague and friend of Thomas Reid, as well as the revered teacher of men like Francis Jeffrey of the *Edinburgh Review*, and Sir William Hamilton.

Having learned from his experience as pastor and as University Professor that, increasingly, religion was the divisive factor, education the factor of unity, Thomas Reid, too, is to be understood as a partisan of that sort of patriotism within the Union which regarded the school system and the Universities as Scotland's central institutions. In his account of the University of Glasgow, he emphasizes, in the Adam Smith manner, the difference between the general and liberal education dispensed in the North, and the more exclusive arrangements of the South. At the same time, Reid is far from being an echo of Adam Smith, and, in his characteristic contributions to the Aberdeen curricular reforms, he unmistakably identified himself with a position of extreme intellectualism – far more characteristic of the Continent than of Britain, and very unlike anything in Adam Smith – which insists that all departments of higher study must converge on, and be crowned by, a central metaphysic of first principles.

Shaken out of his intellectual optimism by the *Treatise of Human Nature*, Reid developed a double-sided attitude to Hume, regarding him as a philosophical critic of consummate genius, and, at the same time, a dangerously unsettling influence. The achievement of Hume was to have brought to light certain fundamental and deep-seated contradictions which the Enlightenment had unthinkingly taken over from the Renaissance and the Middle Ages. The danger inherent in his achievement was that the Humeian presentation of these contradictions as absolute, as rooted in the na-

16

ture of things, played into the hands of the party which regarded human nature as containing an original flaw. What Reid feared about Hume was that Calvinist or as one might say 'Pascalian' vein implicit in the scepticism.

A bold and yet supremely subtle intelligence, Reid directed his attention to the side of Hume from which Adam Smith had prudently held aloof – namely the metaphysical challenge. Was there indeed a sort of antinomy, an ultimate irreconcilability, between Continental intellectualism and English empiricism or pragmatism, as Hume had said, and as Kant, after him, was to agree? Avoiding the German solution of a higher synthesis which includes both, Reid sought a way out by means of a careful *distinctio* which, in these days of Husserl and phenomenology, has a very modern ring. Distinguishing sharply between science and philosophy, he pointed out that the intellectualist or Cartesian approach is true of the latter and false of the former, whereas the experimental or Baconian approach applies to the former, but not the latter. In a word, for Reid, it is the French who understand best about spirit, whereas the English are more at home in matter.

Elucidating the implications of this position for the philosophy of mind, Reid turned away from England and faced towards France. Taking a global view, he pointed out that not merely is there no serious contradiction between the English empiricist inheritance, and Continental Cartesianism, but, rightly regarded, the former is, in pure philosophy, only a sort of variant, an extreme aberration of the latter. Putting himself in a historical perspective, which sees the main stream of philosophical development as by-passing England, he next taught that the philosophical divergence which raised a really serious problem, was the conflict between the inheritance of Aristotle, and the pioneer effort of René Descartes to initiate a new start. Finally, with a cautious glance to the future, Reid looked forward to 'a third age of man' which will advance beyond the second or Cartesian age, in much the same way as the latter was an advance on the first or Aristotelian. The slogan which inspired Reid's criticism of the Renaissance heritage as he prepared for the third age of man, was not, however, (as one might be tempted to think) 'Back to Aristotle', but 'Back to Descartes himself', and to the genuine original inspirations of Cartesianism. In the first place, Descartes was absolutely right in insisting that the philosophy of mind must have recourse to the inward-looking method of reflective analysis. The more external approach of the Aristotelians, Reid thinks, completely denatures mind by employing unscientific analogical methods which result in merely dispositional theories of human self-consciousness, such as compare the intelligence of man to the brittleness of a goblet. But in the second place, if we are to realize where Cartesianism went wrong, betraying its splendid start, it isn't enough to go to Descartes himself; we must also study the writings of his gifted disciples – especially the brilliant debate between Malebranche and Arnaud, which, Reid thinks, reveals, better than any other document, the real nature of the aberration of Europe's intellectual inheritance.

The stimulating sanity of this second version of the Scottish Enlightenment, due to the genius of Reid and

Adam Smith, finally got through to Europe and America in the aftermath of the French Revolution. Welcomed by most countries, these Scottish ideas were nowhere more enthusiastically received than among the French nation, which, apart from the attraction of this novel platform of moderate and forward-looking liberalism, was duly impressed to find that its ancient Scottish allies, in spite of political separation, still remained spiritually faithful. The eighteenth-century Encyclopédistes had been, they now saw, premature in dismissing Scotland as once 'redoubtable' as a nation, but now, since the English Union, 'venal'. Perceiving that the venality was limited to political relations and, so far, did not touch essentials, men like Victor Cousin, Charles de Rémusat, Philarète Chasles made ample amends in their remarkable studies of culture in post-Union Scotland, thus setting in motion an intellectual current which has been splendidly maintained by Emile Boutroux in the 1900 epoch, and M. Maxime Chastaing in our own time.

Berkeley's Impact on Scottish Philosophers

In 1728, when the sixteen-year-old Hume, still apparently 'at college', was beginning, all unknown to his family, to turn his attention to philosophy, Edinburgh and Glasgow were swarming with earnest metaphysicians, many of them not much older than Hume himself. 'It is well known', the Ochtertyre papers relate, 'that between the years 1723 and 1740 nothing was in more request with the Edinburgh literati, both laical and clerical, than metaphysical disquisitions', and Locke, Clarke, Butler and Berkeley are mentioned as the chief subjects for debate. Moreover, it is clear enough from the records that this surge of intellectual interests was chiefly the work of a younger generation, wearied alike of Calvinist theology and of Jacobite politics. Indeed, to begin with, it was the students' societies which took the lead, and a plain enough hint of their serious critical attack is given in one sour entry in the diary of the Calvinist minister Woodrow for 1726. 'These student clubs are like to have a very ill influence; they declare against reading and cry up thinking.'

Of the list of metaphysical themes mentioned as occupying Scottish youth, the most distinctive as well as the best attested is the interest in Berkeley's philosophy. In England, coxcombs might refute Berkeley with a grin, and sages by kicking their foot hard against a stone, but north of the Tweed the paradoxes of immaterialism were taken much more seriously. One of the

Edinburgh student societies – called the Rankenian Club from its having Ranken's Tavern as its meeting place – was especially notable for carrying on a philosophical correspondence with Berkeley himself in the years prior to his departure for Bermuda in 1728. According to a respectable tradition, Berkeley was greatly pleased with the acuteness displayed in these letters and was heard to say that no person understood his system better than this set of young gentleman in north Britain.[1] That of course is as it may be, but it appears indubitable that it was members of the Rankenian Club who first introduced Berkeley into the Scottish curriculum: George Turnbull lecturing on him at Aberdeen in the late twenties, to a student audience containing the youthful Thomas Reid; John Stevenson setting the Edinburgh students, from 1730 onwards, essays on Berkeley which may still be read; and Colin Maclaurin, also in Edinburgh, discussing with his classes in the same decade the more specialised topic of Berkeley's views on physics and mathematical foundations.[2] At the same time Scottish interest in Berkeley was not confined to this group of Rankenian academics, and the first really systematical examination of the Berkeleian theory was done by Andrew Baxter, friend of Lord Kames, in a successful book, entitled *The Nature of the Human Soul*, which went into three editions – 1733, 1737 and 1745 – and which supplied the Edinburgh students with many of the arguments in the essay.

One must not jump to the conclusion that the Scots found Berkeley's immaterialism a congenial doctrine. On the contrary, it made them uneasy because its paradoxes seemed so silly and yet were so difficult to

21

refute. At the same time there were exceptions – notably Smibert, the Edinburgh artist who accompanied Berkeley to the Bermudas, and George Turnbull, the Aberdeen Regent who ultimately abandoned Scotland and the Scottish church for Berkeley's country and Berkeley's church.

To understand the background of Berkeleianism in Scotland, we had best go to two books, *The Principles of Moral Philosophy*,[3] by the said George Turnbull, born in 1698, student at Edinburgh from 1717–1721, and *The Discoveries of Sir Isaac Newton*, by Colin Maclaurin, born also in 1698, educated at Glasgow University and appointed professor of Mathematics in 1725. Turnbull's book indeed was not published till 1740, nor Maclaurin's till 1748, two years after his death, but each book, as it happens, can fairly be claimed as giving some sort of indication of the ideas canvassed in the Rankenian club and University circles before 1728, Turnbull's book being, according to its author's own preface,[4] ultimately based on lectures he gave to students some twelve years earlier (i.e. before 1728) when regent at the Marischal College, Aberdeen, and Maclaurin's book, or at least the part that interests us, namely the first hundred pages, being said by his editor Patrick Murdoch[5] to have been already in existence since about 1728, except for such additions as had been necessary to keep it abreast of new works.

Both Turnbull and Maclaurin advocate the use of Newton's experimental methods in all physical science, and in the cause of this experimentalism, Maclaurin attacks the conceptions of Descartes, Leibnitz and Spinoza. In particular he opposes the pretentions of these philosophers to establish laws of nature *a priori*; and he argues patiently and in detail against the various proofs offered by Descartes and Leibnitz against the inconceivability of a vacuum, following up this argument with briefer objections to their alleged demonstrations by pure reason of laws of continuity and of conservation of force, and ridiculing in between times Spinoza's way of 'assuming a definition of substance and attributes at his pleasure and passing from these definitions as true ideas (as he calls them) to the necessary existence of the thing defined by a pretended immediate consequence which he will not allow to be disputed'.[6] Moreover, he does not leave us in doubt as to his opinion of the major heresy of the rationalist school: 'it is not the business of philosophy to take in at once, in one view, the whole scheme of nature; but to extend with great care and circumspection our knowledge, by just steps, from sensible things as far as our observation or reasonings from them will carry us, in our enquiries concerning either the great motions and operations of nature, or her more subtle and hidden works'.[7] Occupied as he is with polemics against the rival sect, he does not stop to enquire into the philosophical implications of this obligation on us 'to allow the necessity of taking it (nature) in parts and of proceeding with all the care and caution we are capable of in enquiring into each part'. Perhaps, if he had given more time to questions of first principles, he would have developed a doctrine, something like Hume's, of the externality of relations, but the nearest he comes to doing this is his quoting a couple of relevant sentences from Spinoza's *Ethics*, part I, proposition 15 Schol.[8]

By comparison with Maclaurin, Turnbull gives a

somewhat superficial sketch of the principles of empiricism in science. Unlike Maclaurin he does not join issue at all with the continental rationalists.

When it comes to the problems of philosophy proper, both Turnbull and Maclaurin are evidently just as much taken as Hume was with the notion of introducing the method of experimental reasoning into moral subjects, and of thereby doing for the problem of mind what Newton had done for the problem of matter. 'It was', says Turnbull, 'by this important hint (of Newton's) that I was led long ago to apply myself to the study of the human mind in the same way as to that of the human body.'[9] Moral philosophy, he goes on to explain, is distinguished from physiology, because 'it enquires chiefly about objects not perceivable by means of our outward organs of sense, but by internal feeling and experience'.[10] Those introspectable objects too, he goes on, 'may properly be called parts of nature', and in any case 'it is obvious that an enquiry about any of them is a question of natural history or fact'. Maclaurin, too, adopts the same view as Turnbull that the application of the experimental method to mind involves the study of internally experienced facts. 'It is evident', he says, trying to confute some *a priori* speculations of Leibnitz, 'that as it is from internal consciousness I know anything of liberty, so no assertion contrary to what I am conscious of can be admitted; *and it were better perhaps to treat this abstruse subject after the manner of experimental philosophy than to fill a thousand pages with metaphysical discussions of it.*' (Italics mine.)[11]

In the event, neither Turnbull nor Maclaurin devotes much space to this sort of purely philosophical problem, the one being chiefly occupied with Newton's physics, the other with an empiricist approach to theology. However, the interesting thing is that such discussions of 'the human mind' as we do find in them tend to bear out the traditions which have come down respecting the interest of the Rankenian Club.

Of the existence in Turnbull of a certain Berkeleian tendency there can be no reasonable doubt. In his preface[12] he praises Berkeley by name and in his text he follows a procedure very like Berkeley, dismissing the independent material world as an unnecessary entity. 'A material world', he says, 'is to all intents and purposes nothing, when considered as absolutely unperceived' because 'a material world without being perceived would be of no use'.[13] What, he asks, could be said about a material world considered apart from perceptive beings? 'It is neither good nor bad, beautiful nor deformed, useful nor hurtful, it cannot be said to have any property but bare existence which, by consequence, would be in that case thrown away on it.'[14] Finally, he makes explicit these characteristically Berkeleian conclusions that 'enquiries into the material world can only mean enquiries into the effects material laws and connections have on perceptive beings'. Then, by way of postscript he gives a thoroughly Berkeleian analysis of what is meant by speaking of a body as annihilated. 'When matter is said to be destroyed, all that we mean is that perceptive beings have lost a certain class or order of perceptions, conveyed into them from without.'[15] In short, Turnbull like Berkeley, tried to analyse away the commonsense notion of matter as existing independent of perception, or in other words, he wanted to annul the ordinary distinction made in colloquial language between *to be* and *to be perceived*.

Turnbull, however, doesn't follow Berkeley only in his reductive theory of our knowledge of matter, he also takes over Berkeley's commonsense argument in favour of free will. In elucidating this latter topic, Turnbull introduces a principle of respect for ordinary language which is at variance with what he has said on the former topic, in the sense that it would seem to be incompatible with his Berkeleian denial of the colloquial distinction between *esse* and *percipi*. 'Language', says he, 'not being invented by philosophers but contrived to express sentiments or what everyone perceives, we may be morally sure that where universally all languages make a difference there really is in nature a difference.'[16] Armed with this principle, Turnbull condemns utilitarian philosophers for proclaiming in defiance of ordinary language that the right is nothing but the expedient, and then fiercely attacks the sort of determinist who dismisses as nonsensical our everyday talk about 'might have acted otherwise'. 'Common language', he says, 'is built on fact or universal feeling; and to say that such phrases received in all languages and universally understood have no meaning is to assert an absurdity.'[17] Now Turnbull, one might think, should at this point have remembered that Berkeley offered his principle of *esse* is *percipi* as an amendment of general colloquial usage, and he might have gone on to note that the advice of Berkeley on this subject of perception – 'to speak with the vulgar but think with the learned' – is considerably at variance with the rule followed by the same Berkeley in other connections to accept the distinctions of vulgar speech as valid where these distinctions are found in all languages. In fact, however, Turnbull does nothing of the kind, and seems not to have the slightest inkling of any incompatibility between a commonsense ethics and a reductive epistemology.

Colin Maclaurin, in sharp contrast to George Turnbull, makes a very great deal indeed of the inconsistency of Berkeleianism and commonsense in his brief notice of the problem of perception. 'It were easy', he concludes 'to make many more remarks about the philosophy of those whose principles would lead them to maintain that external objects vary with our perceptions and that the object is different when perceived by different minds or by the same mind in different circumstances.'[18]

However, Maclaurin limits himself to making some two or three points against this position. In the first place, this thesis is an unnatural one (i.e. in conflict with commonsense); 'when a figure described on a board', he says, 'produces a similar impression on all who see it, it is as natural to ascribe this to one cause as when we speak to a numerous audience the effect of the discourse is to be ascribed to us.'[19] But in the second place, what about the Berkeleian point that this allegedly commonsense notion of a material substance behind the various sense presentations is the notion of a know-not-what which transcends perception and which as such is quite superfluous? To this, Maclaurin apparently would reply that Berkeley does not regard as superfluous our commonsense notion of other people's minds although these transcend perception too and are not directly knowable. 'As it is not an objection against the existence of the souls of other men that they may be very different from the notion or conception we have formed of them, so it is no just reason against the existence of body that its inner essence or substratum may be very different of anything we know of it.'[20]

Although the Rankenian Club was by all accounts a forum rather than a clique, this utter divergence of view between two of its members is certainly noteworthy. In this connection, the relevant fact probably is that Turnbull left Edinburgh and presumably gave up regular membership of the club in 1722, while Maclaurin did not settle in Edinburgh until 1725 and presumably did not take up with the club before that date. It thus seems a fair surmise that Turnbull's opinions of Berkeley derive from the days of the club's initial enthusiasm, and Maclaurin's from the time of the club's final disillusionment which is hinted at in the account in the *Scots Magazine*. Interestingly, however, it is also a fact that during the years between the departure of the one from Edinburgh and the arrival of the other there, both these men were colleagues on the teaching staff of the Marischal College, Aberdeen, and it is accordingly quite likely that they may have argued about Berkeley there.

Philosophically speaking, the importance of Turnbull and Maclaurin is that, both born in 1698 and both appointed very early to Aberdeen professorships in the room of expelled Jacobites, they were among the advance guard of the generation which was to produce the Humes and the Reids. In the case of Reid certainly, the fact of direct influence can hardly be doubted. In the first place, he almost certainly got from his teacher

Turnbull not only his passing belief in Berkeleianism but also his lifelong respect for colloquial distinctions. But secondly, Maclaurin's widely read book published in 1748 indubitably illumines and may well have influenced the crisis in Reid's career – about forty years prior to 1785 – which made him aware of the difficulty of combining a Berkeleian theory of perception with this principle of ordinary language. Thus, at the very end of Maclaurin's general introduction to his *Newton* we encounter a memorable version of the stereotype which Reid was to propagate to posterity, about Berkeley's philosophy as inevitably leading to the Humean scepticism. 'In forming these systems', Maclaurin says, meaning both the rationalist continental system and the sense datum system of British empiricism, 'he who has prosecuted each of them furthest has done the valuable service that, while he vainly imagined he had completed or improved it, he really opened up the fallacy and reduced it to absurdity. Many who suffered themselves to be pleased with Descartes' fables were put to a stand by Spinoza's impieties and some, willing to give up the reality of matter, would not think of giving up their own and other minds.'[21]

Reid, then, was influenced by the Rankenians, but what of Hume? Here the story current in circles close to Hume speaks of the Rankenian Club if not as influencing, at least as anticipating Hume's *reductio ad absurdum* of the Berkeleian empiricism. What other meaning can be attached to the reminiscence of Robert Wallace (born 1697), a founder member of the Rankenian Society, that in their discussions of Berkeley the Rankenians had been already engaged in 'pushing his amazing tenets all the lengths they have been carried in subsequent publications'?[22] This, no doubt, is a large claim but it isn't difficult to show that there was very probably something in it. Go to the essays produced by the students of John Stevenson, the Rankenian member who was Logic professor at Edinburgh, or go to the book by Andrew Baxter which the students drew heavily upon for their essays. Compare what is said there with what Turnbull and Maclaurin were saying, and it will soon become evident that the standard of argumentation attained is well worthy to be regarded as anticipating even David Hume.

Turnbull might not have noticed that Berkeley's views on perception contradict common language as much as common sense, but Andrew Baxter in 1733 was perfectly aware of this fact. It is, Baxter argues, a humbug on Berkeley's part to claim that his attack is directed only against the metaphysician's talk about material substance and not against the plain man's talk about bodies.[23] Berkeley 'supposes that the term [to exist] hath the same import when applied to corporeal things as the term *to be perceived*',[24] asserting (strongly indeed) that the word existence is otherwise unintelligible. 'Whence it clearly follows that, for Berkeley, matter which is not perceived doth not exist.' But, Baxter continues, 'the artificer seems to understand that his tools exist all the intermediate time, after he lays them by at night till he takes them up the next morning'.[25]

If we bear in mind here Turnbull's Berkeleian analysis of what it means to speak of annihilation, we at once become aware of the implicit intellectual tension between him and Baxter. The former insists on giving

30

a strictly phenomenalist interpretation of the notion of non-existence, the latter on the other hand is urging the counter-position that this kind of redefinition tampers in a mystificatory way with a basic distinction of ordinary language.

If sometimes, as here, we get an argument in the style of Reid which appeals to ordinary language, elsewhere the case against Berkeley is formulated in a Humean manner in terms of the slogan of 'natural belief'. Take the following extract from an Edinburgh Logic class essay[26] dated 16th May 1740: 'We observe all mankind to be governed by the same principle (of belief in externality), and even the philosopher, in spite of any refinement of speculation, to pursue the same conduct as the peasant.' But what then of the standard Berkeleian retort which was employed above by Turnbull that this notion of an external world was an unnecessary entity which ought to be slashed off by Occam's razor? The student however does not allow himself to be put off by this challenge and counters it in a spirit of Calvinist severity. 'Supposing the ideal system (i.e. Berkeley's immaterialism) to be admitted, it would, it is claimed, make no difference to us. But this species of scepticism, as it leads us from our constitution, and puts us under a different principle, ought to be considered as an unnatural state of mind wherein, the just order and balance of things being lost, it is necessarily succeeded by great uneasiness and many anxieties which are no other than the strong efforts of nature to restore and recover herself to her former and original condition, as also they may serve to admonish the soul of the impropriety of its doubts and in that measure dispose it to obeying το Θειον or the law of its constitution.' – In this way the Berkeleian appeal to a pragmatic criterion is answered on its own grounds. The practical effects of the *esse-percipi*, far from facilitating thought, induce, in a shattering experience, the rediscovery of a world of 'natural beliefs'.

Just as in this passage on the connection of 'belief' with the 'balance of the sentiments', the position of the student is exactly that of David Hume on pages 185–186 of the Selby-Bigge *Treatise*, so too the language of the Logic class essay runs parallel to Hume's in its preliminary 'exposition' of Berkeley's theory. On page 189 of the same book we read 'a single perception can never produce the idea of a double existence', etc. John Carre's essay on Berkeley speaks the same language. 'The notion of a double perception, one of the idea (i.e. idea of sense) and another of the object, being attended with great absurdity, it necessarily resolved itself into a single perception with an unknown and unperceived object, or rather the same idea considered under different respects as existing in the mind, and as existing in something external and not perceived; which words have either no meaning at all, or they must express a manifold and downright contradiction; for what greater repugnance can there be than to suppose solid movable extension perceived to exist unperceived, or what is the same thing to suppose an idea to be unperceived or something not perceived to be an idea.'

Using the same language as Hume, the student nevertheless repudiates Berkeley where Hume accepts him. 'Even our sight informs us not of distance or outness (so to speak) immediately.' (Hume's *Treatise* p. 191) 'The idea of outness, I know', says the student, 'is by the asserters of this new philosophy alleged to be acquired, and in consequence to be no original perception, but as these have few instances where the observation could be justly made, therefore, no great credit is to be given to the fact.'

Just as John Carre throws light on the question whether or not visual experience supports the *esse-percipi*, so too Baxter's book helps us to understand a most interesting but too often neglected passage in Hume in which the point at issue is whether the facts of tactual experience bear out Berkeleianism. In the *Treatise*, pp. 230–231, Hume asks whether the tactual experience of feeling a solid body involves a single perception or a double perception in the sense explained.[27] Is there 'a feeling or sensation' 'conjoined with the solidity'? To this question Hume's reply would seem in principle to be that 'my hand reveals to me the resistance of objects, their hardness or softness, but not *itself*'. But on the other hand Baxter before him, as Reid after him, exerted all his ingenuity to find a case which on the contrary made it plain that this sort of experience involves not a single but a double perception. Suppose, says Baxter, 'a man in a dark night were groping out his way with a long pole in his hand and felt something to resist it,[28] is it not the case that he would indubitably have the experience of two things, the pole and the resisting obstacle?

The students make a great deal, and justifiably, of one particular passage in which Baxter makes a very good attempt indeed to establish as against Berkeley that tactual experience really does contain a double perception in Reid's sense of a sensation of touch combined with a perception of touch. Baxter, followed by Gilbert Mathison and by Francis Garden, fastens onto the rhetorical question asked by Berkeley in *Principles* para. 4: What are houses, mountains, etc., but things we perceive by sense, and what are things we perceive by sense but sensations or ideas? There is, says Baxter, followed by the two students, a contradiction here. In the first place, mountains, houses, etc., are things we perceive with the help of sense organs, but sensations are not experienced with the help of sense organs. Secondly, 'a sensation may become the object to a reflective act of mind, yet it is not then the object to itself'.[29] That is to say, in our ordinary perceptions of houses, mountains, etc., we are extroverted and in consequence can't notice our 'sensations'. In this way, Baxter and the boys in their criticisms of Berkeley point towards the distinction between sensation and perception which Thomas Reid was later to exploit.[30]

To round off this discussion of the role of the Rankenian Club, we had better face up to the question often raised in these last years – especially in Harry M. Bracken's lively book on 'the early reception of immaterialism' – as to how far Berkeley's philosophy was misunderstood by its first Scottish votaries. In such matters, no doubt, it is necessary to proceed with caution, but at the same time on the basis of the fresh evidences which we have unfolded, it begins to appear as if Berkeley was not after all so much a misunderstood philosopher as we have been led to suppose. In the first place, consider carefully the line of argument which is touched upon both in Turnbull and in Baxter as to the compatibility of the principle of *esse-percipi* with the rule which enjoins respect for the distinctions of ordinary language. The important point here is that Turnbull certainly seems to have a fairly good grasp of the point which Mr Bracken says was generally misunderstood, viz. that 'on Berkeley's empirical meaning criterion the very definition of matter is inconsistent'. The proof of this is that Turnbull in his remarks on annihilation is subtle enough to make the sort of move which the most reliable interpreters of Berkeley, especially J. F. Ferrier, have marked down as the index of a profound understanding of immaterialism – the move, viz. of insisting on giving a phenomenalist interpretation not merely to existence but to non-existence, not merely to *esse* but to *non-esse*. Even Berkeley himself, as Ferrier pointed out, was occasionally unfaithful to his own principles, when judged by this strict criterion. Hence on what is perhaps the most ultimate criterion one can get on this topic – Berkeley's understanding of his own system – Turnbull seems to emerge with some credit. As to Baxter, on the other hand, it doesn't surely matter so much whether or not, as Mr Bracken says, he fully understood Berkeley's logical point about the inconsistency of the definition of matter, since Baxter himself, as his remarks about Berkeleianism and ordinary language show, was on his side acutely aware of the difficulty, to which Berkeley himself was apparently blind, of both laying down the rule of speaking with the vulgar and at the same time admitting the *esse-percipi*.

In the second place, the high standard of the Scottish arguments also emerges in the debate over Berkeley of which we have found traces not only in Baxter and in Professor Stevenson's Logic class essays but also in Hume and Reid as to whether the fact of my visual experience of a body or my tactual experience of it is capable of being analysed as a double perception or whether one can find nothing but a single perception. In this case, the common focus of these various discussions would seem pretty certainly to be the pages in Berkeley's First Dialogue where Hylas and Philonous discuss whether visual or tactual experience permits of a distinction between sensation on the one hand and object of sensation on the other. Clearly enough the Scots have taken Berkeley's point pretty well, and much instruction is still to be got from their arguments, pro and con, as to the possibility of drawing this sort of distinction within experience.

Thirdly, we want to draw attention to the line of argumentation which we found in Maclaurin. The feature of Berkeley which he objects to is what we should now call the reductionism – the attempt, that is, to treat statements about a material object as being nothing but statements about a certain multiplicity of actual and possible sense data. No doubt it is possible to challenge the fairness of Maclaurin's interpretation of Berkeley, but at the same time it is obviously far from being wildly wrong and is in any ordinary sense of the term a perfectly tenable position. As to whether Maclaurin was right in treating Berkeley's philosophy as simply a halfway house to Hume, that of course is another matter and one which could be discussed endlessly. The important point to make here is surely that even if Maclaurin may have been in some sense unfair to Berkeley in tying him up with Hume, nevertheless this fateful error, if it was indeed an error, was one which in some sense opened a whole long, intellectual epoch and in that way may be accounted creative. It cannot possibly be dismissed, then, as a petty blunder indicative of low intellectual standards. On the contrary it has to be ranked as nothing less than the momentous decision, backed by the posthumous authority of the man who was Newton's chief disciple, and published in a kind of memorial volume which had a most extensive and imposing subscription list, that henceforward the reductive species of sense-data empiricism which was arising in Britain must be regarded as being, from the point of view of serious philosophy, just as extravagant and inacceptable as the line of continental rationalism which had been developed by Spinoza. No doubt there was something overhasty in Maclaurin's tactic of identifying Berkeley as a propounder of this reductive positivism, but at the same time this much must be said on Maclaurin's behalf that Berkeley himself does not seem to have done enough in his writings to put his readers on their guard against this interpretation of his intentions.

The effect of these three lines of argument is then to corroborate the story which was handed down not only by Robert Wallace's son in *The Scots Magazine* memoir of his father which we have cited but also by Dugald Stewart in two or three careful and considered references he makes to Professor John Stevenson. 'The influence of this society (the Rankenian) in encouraging the kind of philosophical research which has since become so fashionable in Scotland, has often been mentioned to me by those who have the best opportunities of observing the rise and progress of Scottish literature.'[31] Since the thing ultimately at stake in this matter was nothing less than the intellectual honour of his country, Dugald Stewart is very emphatic about informing us of his sources for such a claim. 'The authority I allude to is that of my old friend and preceptor Dr John Stevenson who was himself a member of the Rankenian club and was accustomed to mention that fact in his *Academical Prelections*.'[32] The point which Stewart was so careful about putting over was one which, it is clear, he considered of the utmost importance to anyone who wanted to understand the reason why, throughout the eighteenth century, culture in Scotland had become so markedly different from the sort of intellectual interests which were prevalent south of the Tweed. The great differentiating fact had been that, whereas Berkeley had fallen flat in England, his point had been enthusiastically and intelligently taken in the north. The ultimate testimony in this matter, Stewart tells us, would seem to go back to Berkeley himself. According to the story which Stevenson as well as Wallace had publicly vouched for, the members of the Rankenian society were 'said to have been numbered by the Bishop of Clone among the few who understood the scope of his reasonings against the existence of matter'.[33]

Notes

1. See article on Wallace in *Scots Magazine*, July 1771.
2. The list of Rankenian members in Woodhouselee's Life of Lord Kames contains besides the three names mentioned, also those of Smibert, Robert Wallace, Boswell's father, and two friends of Hume, Sir Alexander Dick and Sir Andrew Mitchell. In a letter to Hume in 1764, Dick speaks of their association with Mitchell as having happened a great while ago.
3. Turnbull's book was published by John Noon, also responsible for the original volume of the *Treatise of Human Nature*. The two books are mentioned side by side in the publishers' list on the end page of Vol. 2 of Turnbull's book.
4. p. xii, Vol. 1.
5. p. vi of the 1748 edition.
6. *Loc. cit.*, p. 78.

7. *Loc. cit.*, p. 19.
8. *Loc. cit.*, p. 75.
9. p. iii, Vol. 1 of Turnbull.
10. p. 9, Vol. 1 of Turnbull.
11. p. 83 of Maclaurin.
12. See Vol. 1 of Turnbull, p. viii and pp. 3 and 4.
13. Vol. 1, p. 408.
14. Vol. 1, pp. 433 and 434.
15. Vol. 1, pp. 232 and 233. For completeness add also the longer reference in Vol. 2, pp. 22 and 23.
16. Vol. 1, p. 118.
17. Vol. 1, p. 16.
18. p. 99 of Maclaurin.
19. Also p. 99 of Maclaurin.
20. p. 98 of Maclaurin.
21. p. 95 of Maclaurin.
22. *Scots Magazine, loc. cit.*
23. See *The Nature of the Human Soul*, Vol. 2 of the 1737 edition, in the long footnote pp. 294-297.
24. pp. 294 and 295 of the text of *The Nature of the Human Soul*.
25. See *loc. cit.*
26. This bound manuscript volume which is in Edinburgh University Library came from the Laing collection. I am indebted to the late C. P. Finlayson, the Keeper of Manuscripts, for bringing it to my notice.
27. For the elucidation of the point at issue as it affected Hume and Reid, see my article in *Revue Internationale de Philosophie*, No. 20, from which some paragraphs have been transferred to the present article.
28. Baxter, Vol. 2, p. 291.
29. Baxter, Vol. 2, pp. 288 and 289.
30. The complicated question of Reid's relation to Berkeley can be properly discussed only by someone who, in addition to studying both Berkeley and Reid, also studies their Cartesian predecessors and their Scottish successors, especially Ferrier. See Maxime Chastaing's sequence of five articles, three on the Cartesians (*Rencontres* 1949, *Revue Philosophique* 1951, *ibid.* 1953) followed by the *Berkeley* (*ibid.* 1953) and culminating in the very remarkable *Reid and the Philosophy of Common Sense* (*ibid.* 1954).
31. pp. 105 and 106 of Vol. 10 of Stewart's works, edited Hamilton.
32. *Loc. cit.*, p. xiv (footnote).
33. *Loc. cit.*, p. 106.

Berkeley, Hume, and the Central Problem of Scottish Philosophy

I

How much the development of Scottish philosophy owes to an earlier Irish Enlightenment is often overlooked. Berkeley, of course, is recognized as providing an Irish dimension to eighteenth-century British thought, but so too does Francis Hutcheson, and central ideas of each come together in the former's *Alciphron* (1732). *Alciphron* is Berkeley's critical and systematic challenge to the radical reductivist empiricism produced in an effort to make Locke consistent with himself, to the aestheticism of Shaftesbury's moral philosophy, and to the cynical economism of Mandeville's 'private vices, public virtues' view of social philosophy. Hutcheson, from northern Irish Presbyterian roots, was gradually led by his own concerns with these same elements to shift from the monographic approaches of his early works *(Inquiry concerning Beauty and Virtue,* 1725; *Essay on the Passions and Affections, With Illustrations on the Moral Sense,* 1728) to provide a systematic response to them in his *Compendium* of 1742.

In the last analysis, the creative element in this Irish Enlightenment, the element responsible for preparing the way for the classical period of Scottish philosophy, consisted not only in the parallel pioneering by both Berkeley and Hutcheson, with system-building as the proper way to answer the free thinkers, but also, and more importantly, in the very sharp and stimulating tension between the syntheses constructed or outlined by the two Irish philosophers as the proper way out of the difficulty. Agreeing with one another about the excesses of the new economics, Berkeley and Hutcheson differed radically on the respective values of Shaftesburian ethics and radical empiricism as components in the system that was to check the errors of the *Fable of the Bees* while at the same time preserving its more valuable insights. Berkeley had no sympathy whatever for Shaftesbury's aestheticist brand of ethics or for the common-sense intuitionism it implied, but he saw much promise in the atomistic reductionism and the egoistic utilitarianism of the free-thinking empiricism, provided that it was accompanied and offset, in a dualistic way, by a revival of a metaphysically-minded rationalism modelled on Cartesianism. Hutcheson, on the other hand, had the strongest objection to the utilitarianism-reductivism of the free thinkers, as well as to the Cartesian rationalism added to the mixture by Berkeley as a corrective; but by contrast he saw great promise, epistemological as well as ethical, in Shaftesbury's appeal to the intuitions of common sense, provided that they could be broadened in such a way as to free them from their aestheticist exclusiveness. Already, in the Dublin of the late twenties, the opposition had thus begun to emerge between the contrasting positions that in their tension provided Scottish philosophy with its central problem: the Berkeleian system, according to which, in the interests of reconciling progress with traditional standards, we are to set aside the instincts of the farmer in favour of the sophistication of the philosopher and to think with

41

the learned while we talk with the vulgar; and the Hutchesonian system, according to which, with the same aim of reconciling material advance with the intellectual principle, we are to respect the instincts of the farmer as against the sophistication of the philosopher and initiate a sort of dialogue between the vulgar and the learned, instead of talking down to the farmer from the standpoint of the philosopher.

Understood in these terms, the intellectual divergence between the principal protagonists of the Irish Enlightenment already contains implicitly the central problem of the classical Scottish philosophy; and in this matter I am inclined to think that Sir James Mackintosh was perfectly right when he claimed that the two great Irish philosophers may be said 'to have co-operated in calling forth the metaphysical genius of Scotland,' in the sense that 'though Hutcheson spread the taste and formed the principles' of what was to be called the Scottish philosophy of common sense, Berkeley, by his attacks on common sense and intuitionism, 'undoubtedly produced the scepticism of Hume which stimulated the intuitive school into activity.'[1] As Hume makes clear, Berkeley's function in regard to Scottish philosophy was the purely negative one of shaking to its foundations, by means of his deadly arguments, the common-sense philosophy put over by Hutcheson in Glasgow and eagerly seized on by the Scots as the answer to the great problem of reconciling the old ethics with the new economics. Carried on against a Scottish background, the conflict of principle between these two philosophers 'stimulates a series of major systems in which the problem of the relation of ethics to economics is approached through the fundamentally epistemological issue of the relation between vulgar common sense and philosophical reason.

II

In *Alciphron,* Dialogue 1, Berkeley asserts that the fundamental direction of the free-thinking movement, despite its claims to be deistic and to that extent spiritual, is toward putting modern society on a secularistic basis. Consistently carried out, the experimental or Lockeian approach to knowledge, though it has made possible great advances in physical science, leaves no room for such transcendental and metaphysical entities as God. 'Atheism,' Berkeley has his free thinker say, 'that bugbear of women and fools, is the very type and perfection of free thinking.'[2] In Dialogue 2 he takes up Mandeville's view that austerity, self-sacrifice, or thrift, whatever value they may have had in the stagnant society of a simpler age, are irrelevant in the new age of plenty. To Berkeley, the major weakness in this view is not the implicit hedonism—he does not quarrel with the claim that self-love is an active principle of man's nature—but rather the unenlightened nature of this hedonism. Mandeville's one-sided valuation of excessive consumption overlooks the fact that moderate consumption will do more for the growth of trade than will excessive consumption; the drink trade is cited as an example.

In Dialogue 3 Berkeley reveals that he is largely in agreement with the Shaftesburian view that a consumer society of the Mandevillian type can at best give only a very partial and unstable satisfaction of human needs. But although Berkeley agrees with Shaftesbury that 'the mind of man attaineth to the highest nature of beauty, excellence and perfection, by contemplating the fitness and order of the parts of the moral system, knit together by mutual sympathies,' he finds Shaftesbury's conception of the moral sense to be far too elitist to turn sensual and worldly-minded men to virtue.[3] Lacking, suggests Berkeley, are the 'hope of reward and fear of punishment' which are 'highly expedient to cast the balance of pleasant and profitable on the side of virtue and [are] thereby conducive to the benefit of human society.'[4] In short, in Berkeley's opinion the competing elements of Mandeville's economism and Shaftesbury's aestheticism cannot be reconciled in a social ideal flexible enough to combine comeliness of lifestyle with improved standards of living *unless* the experimentalist-scientific approach presupposed by these rival ethics can be shown to have transcendental-religious implications that have escaped the notice of both proponents. At this point, in Dialogue 4, Berkeley introduces another important theme in the Irish-Scottish debate on free thinking, namely, his own philosophy of the divine visible language. Empiricism, properly refined and reformulated, far from undercutting belief in God, becomes the foundation of a new, perceptually-based proof of Divine existence sufficiently cogent to satisfy Alciphron himself.

The key to the issue is to be found, we are told, in the *New Theory of Vision,* where Berkeley had revealed the phenomenological difference between an object of touch and an object of sight. Locke and traditional philosophy had considered sight and touch as different ways of presenting the same body; for Berkeley they are separate and quite independent modes of experience that nevertheless function together in a kind of organic unity, with visual experiences, strictly analyzed, constituting a form of language by which nature speaks to us about what lies ahead. Berkeley then concludes by claiming that this doctrine of 'divine visible language' implicit in the *New Theory of Vision* constitutes a perceptually-based proof of the existence of God, analogous to our perceptually-based proof, via social experience, of the existence of other minds.

III

In Dublin Francis Hutcheson had made similar criticisms of Mandeville and had in fact anticipated Berkeley's charge of the elitism of the moral sense by 'democratizing,' as W. R. Scott puts it, Shaftsbury's ethics.[5] The all-important insights into the beauty of virtue, he insists, are possible for all men, are at least as possible for the honest farmer as for the virtuoso and are best established, perhaps, by an appeal to a consensus of the farmer as a representative of the vulgar, and the virtuoso as representative of the learned. And not only did Hutcheson anticipate Berkeley's challenge to Shaftesbury, he anticipated and found wanting Berkeley's solution to the foundation of morals. Hutcheson was not the man to be impressed by the fantastic exclusiveness of a metaphysical ethic that cuts off visual perception from its natural connection with tactual perception in order to constitute it the vehicle of some sort of public communing with the provident spirit of God. Instead of making a mystification of the visual sense that would represent the moral consciousness as a sort of Malebranchian listening-in

45

to God, Hutcheson in direct opposition to Berkeley demystifies the latter's theory of vision as a first step in evolving a moderately common-sense view of mind. This brings the moral consciousness down from heaven to earth without returning to the heresy of the free thinkers, reducing the theoretical to the practical, or merging the spiritual and the material. In a letter of 1727 Hutcheson (as also Leibniz and Husserl) maintained that the Berkeleian denial of the common-sense connection between the visual and tactual experience of bodily shapes holds good only if we incongruously compare a 'groping' experience of moving the feeling hand over an object with a static, fixed-eye experience in which the shapes under observation, cubes or spheres, are looked at through one constant angle of vision.[6] But, Hutcheson insists, the paradox of the *New Theory of Vision* is instantly dissolved as soon as we compare the experience of feeling around the contours of an object – in a series of progressive explorations – with the *activity* of a visual observation. In short, by keeping the eye on the move we are able to discover that the variety of successive visual perceptions is similar to the variety of successive tactual perceptions, Thus, confronted with the Berkeleian claim that a so-called visual sphere has, empirically speaking, as little in common with a tangible sphere as it has with a tangible cube, Hutcheson answers by drawing attention to the distinction that, whereas a single glance at a visible sphere may reveal no respect in which it is more like a tangible sphere than a tangible cube, a succession of views of the visible sphere, from different perspectives, will reveal that it corresponds closely to the sphere revealed by successive tactual explorations.

In attacking in this way the *New Theory of Vision*, which was so important to Berkeley as the foundation of his theological ethic, Hutcheson anticipated in outline the insight that was to prove so fundamental and fruitful for the entire Scottish school down to its final creative period in the 1840s: Berkeley's arbitrary separation of the sense fields of sight and touch inevitably makes nonsense of our natural common-sense beliefs of perception, whereas, by contrast, a modern restatement of the traditional view of the two external senses as connected in the sense of being parallel or complementary not only brings us back to common sense in the current acceptation but, more importantly enables us to restore and deepen the original meaning of the phrase 'common sense' as it occurs in the Aristotelean philosophy. Thus Hutcheson, in his argument with Berkeley in Ireland hits upon the vein of intersensorial speculation that was to be one of the chief inspirations of the Scottish philosophy of common sense. His analysis does not approach the profundity of later Scottish philosophers such as Smith, Reid, and Ferrier;[7] nevertheless, he is already, right at the beginning, fully master of the central insight at the basis of all these later insights, namely that Berkeley's idealist paradoxes are the result of his excessive severance of touch from sight and that the common sense of perception calls for a more enhanced role for the instinctive affinity of the two senses than Berkeley gives and for a correspondingly diminished role for the effect of more external association as the thing holding them together. Stimulated by the brilliant originality of what the world considered Berkeley's metaphysical perversity, this northern Irishman whose intellect had been

47

formed in the renaissance of classical standards then under way in the Scottish universities – and not the least by the mathematical and philosophical lessons of his Glasgow teachers Robert Simson and Gershom Carmichael, both of European eminence – thus opened in Dublin the line of inquiry that the Scottish philosophy of common sense was to follow with such distinguished results.

IV

If we are to assess aright Hume's response to the criticism made of the *Fable of the Bees* by both Berkeley and Hutcheson it is essential to bear in mind that appropriately enough to the privileged position of organized learning and of systematic argument in the Scottish way of life of the time, Hume's grasp of Mandeville's thesis considerably surpassed that of the Irish masters who were making such an impression on him. Appreciating the deeper side of what Mandeville said about the division of labor and its advantages, Hume went beyond Hutcheson and Berkeley in understanding that the value of the exchange economy became palpable to the producers engaged in it only gradually when the slow course of experience made them aware that the overall long-term economic benefit to society as a whole was the unintended consequence of the extension of a specialization that had arisen and developed in a haphazard manner prompted by local short-term arrangements. Furthermore, Hume is noteworthy for seeing even more clearly than did Mandeville himself that the system of equality before the law, necessary to the smooth working of the exchange and specialization system does not require, as Hutcheson had thought, a concerted effort of warmhearted public-spiritedness, kept alive from pulpits and professorial chairs, to maintain its efficaciousness and even to bring it into being as a system of justice. Like the division-of-labour system with which it is so closely connected, equality before the law emerges as an accepted public institution only as the unintended consequence of a slow growth of the habit of piecemeal accommodation between individual participants in exchanges having nothing more in view than the narrow aim of mutual convenience. Stressing the thesis that the system of justice 'comprehending the interests of each individual,' though 'of course advantageous to the public, ... [was] not intended for that purpose by its inventors,' Hume goes on in the sequel to denounce Hutcheson's idea that competitive individualism will not work in the interests of society as a whole unless a warmhearted morality of benevolence intervenes to check the inherent tendency to social divisiveness by ensuring due enforcement of the principles of justice appropriate to a commercial society.[8] Properly understood, the provocative slogan of 'private vices, public benefits' contains the great truth, misunderstood by Hutcheson, that the principles of justice insuring the kind of equitable distribution appropriate to the productive system are brought into being and maintained, without any need for the preaching of public morality, by an analogous operation of the principle of unintended consequences that is also responsible for the spontaneous slow development of the division-of-labour system into the accepted principle of public economy. Without denying outright the reality of moral standards, Hume goes on to argue that the concerted efforts to generate enthusiasm for public morality are not, as Hutcheson seems to think, essential to the reconciliation of economic growth with the standards of civilization. Replying to Hutcheson's criticism of the point Hume indicated that it would not be proper to introduce passages in praise of the beauty of virtue – passages meant to encourage the cultivation of public-spiritedness – in a book such as *A Treatise of Human Nature*, the aim of which is to try to bring to notice the sense in which the all-round social development of the standards of justice is, in the last analysis, less the result of planning and of moralistic intervention than of a sort of *laissez faire*.[9] Hutcheson no doubt thinks otherwise, but this is a topic which, as Hume jokingly points out in his letter of 1743, they will always be divided about.

At this point however, there occurs one of these turnabouts in Hume's philosophy that have been so little understood.[10] After having explained at length the sense in which Mandeville is right and Hutcheson wrong, he abruptly proceeds to make clear the sense in which Hutcheson is right and Mandeville is wrong. Hutcheson, Hume says, was not wrong in upholding against Mandeville the fact of a moral sense – so far as it is constituted by my judgment as an impartial spectator, made possible by sympathy, upon the conduct of others and by my detached judgment upon myself – as coming about indirectly by my sympathetic identification with the sympathetic reaction of the spectators to myself. Where Hutcheson erred was in failing to see that the social role to be attributed to conscience is not moralistic, as an inspirer of public-spiritedness, but primarily and essentially logical or intellectual, as making possible the metaphysical self-transcendence essential to the impartiality of mind, required by science as well as by justice. As understood by Hume, Hutcheson's and Berkeley's problem of how to prevent a clash between Mandeville's program of economic growth and the standard of civilization is, so far as it is real, less a problem of morals and of moralizing, let alone theology, than a problem of knowledge – a problem even of producing systematic textbooks of scientific method that could be used as a vehicle of enlightenment.

Putting together the two points of view that Hutcheson had set against one another, Hume thus sees society's development as an interconnected operation at two levels. What he means is that the intellectual traffic in ideas and theory that criticizes and modifies specialized production grows up side by side with the traffic in wares, being made possible by this latter. Originally not an object of distinct consciousness on its own account, the intellectual element in the social process, according to Hume, emerges on the view of the participants as a separate department, only when, with the growth of the community in size and complexity, the developments in the sciences and the arts and law cannot be carried through without a sufficient element of the free criticism of inherited taboos.[11] In a series of stimulating essays outlining his views on the sociology of knowledge,[12] Hume argues that in this conscious emergence of the intellectual side of the process as a relatively independent department, 'according to the necessary progress of things,'[13] law must precede science. First, the growth of the division of labour at least so far as concerns the rise of the 'vulgar arts ... of commerce and manufacture,'[14] creates the conditions for the rise of justice and law as a public institution. Subsequently, the mutual criticism and argument about the nature and application of laws that occurs in free societies[15] prepares the way for the higher branches of science such as philosophy and ethics, as well as for the exact sciences, which, beginning on an informal, trial and error basis, become established and institutionalized forms only when experience has enabled society to appreciate their relevance. Still building on Mandeville's foundations, but reconciling them with Hutcheson's ideas about the fundamental role of impartiality and detachment in civilization, Hume elaborates his vision of the development of the economy, law, and the sciences as interconnected elements in the spontaneous 'ferment' that constitutes civilization.[16]

On the view I am taking it seems probable that the new 'scene of thought,' which Hume himself (as he reports in the Letter to a Physician) had found so overwhelming, arose from his sudden glimpse of the possibility that Mandeville's modern world of individualism far from being incompatible with Hutcheson's social-minded doctrine, could not fulfill itself in the process of economic growth unless the individuals in question, in addition to their involvement with one another in the process of specialized production for exchange and profit, were also united with one another in a web of mutual sympathy or communication. By enabling each to enter into the other's point of view, this union made it possible for them to 'see themselves as others see them,' and thereby to acquire the sense of objectivity indispensable to the science and the justice required by an advanced economy. Without in the least denying Mandeville's *laissez faire* thesis that 'through the joint labour of many ages' institutions 'grow up in an unplanned way' that reconciles men's divergent interests, Hume goes on to challenge the implication that 'the creation of even laws' that are to function as the rule for a given market society are brought about solely through the interplay of selfish interests and altogether apart from social feelings. On the other hand it would be impossible for the laws regulating commercial transactions and for the scientific standards required by a commercial society to become socially realized if the sympathetic identification with one's competitors – and also with disinterested third-party spectators – did not make it possible for the participants in the social process to become aware of their social blind spots and moral biases (in much the same way as one is able in sense perception to detect the illusions of a given sense by comparing its point of view with that of the other senses relevant to the situation). In this way Hume brings together Hutcheson's point about the analogy between the intersensorial and the interpersonal.[17]

But just at the very point where Hume seems to have brought to its full maturity the Hutchesonian project of a common-sense philosophy of progress by reconciling it with the Mandeville theory of free development that Hutcheson had found ethically unacceptable, there suddenly occurs a second and even more surprising turnabout. In responding to the strange and almost unearthly insights of Bishop Berkeley, Hume begins to subject the enlightenment philosophy, to which he has himself given a classic formulation, to a skeptical critique of an equally classic character that, down to the present day, has perhaps never been adequately answered. Introducing the crisis of science he sees lurking beneath the surface of the movement of Western civilization as thus sketched, Hume starts from the point that the verification process, inseparable from the growth of science and law that guarantees continued progress, involves as a necessary component a social dimension (unnoticed by Cartesian individualism) constituted by the 'sympathetic' communication of viewpoints between one leading section of the community and another. This makes possible the element of critical self-detachment essential to the maintenance of standards in the master science of philosophy and in the special sciences. At first sight, Hume goes on, this new sense of the social foundations of science bears a promising aspect for the present venture of civilization. As he points out in the piece written originally to introduce his essays as a whole,[18] the eighteenth century is witnessing a developing dialogue between the learned and the conversable – between the experts and the liberal-minded part of the laity – that is raising the intellectual standard of both parties and thus of society as a whole. This alters entirely the situation pertaining hitherto when, as the result of the intellectual barrier between the sections, the learned lost touch with practical life and wandered in merely speculative generalities, while the liberal laity could not rise above the particular and the inessential. Instead of taking an interest in history, poetry, politics, and even philosophy (at least, the easier parts) the laity occupied themselves with gossip and chitchat.

Overcoming the atomizing sectionalization that had for centuries restrained progress, the ferment of public discussion characteristic of Western society in modern times not only enables the march of progress to reattain the classic heights it had reached in the best days of the Greeks and the Romans, but it seems to hold out the hope of building an even more durable civilization, in proportion as the guiding idea of philosophy since the Renaissance has a promise of surpassing in depth and solidity the philosophy by which ancient civilization steered itself.[19]

At the same time, in spite of these favorable prognostications, Hume was concerned to point out in his sociology of knowledge that there could be difficulties ahead for the progress of civilization. Formulating a principle of the inequality or peculiarity of cultural developments among the various peoples constituting the spearhead of Western enlightenment, he argues that, owing to the unfathomably complicated conditions involved in the rise of cultures, they all suffer in one way or another from different intellectual weaknesses, either blind spots in their cultures or shallowness of their social bases. Thus, while there is no doubt a close connection between the rise of the vulgar arts of commerce and manufacture, on the one hand, and that of a properly constituted system of justice and equality before the law, on the other, there does not by any means seem to be so close a connection between a country's achievement of this combination of economics with justice and its subsequent appearance before the world as a hotbed of higher culture and science. Free societies such as Holland, despite the advanced state of their economy and their law, are nevertheless backward in literature and philosophy; and the English, too, notwithstanding their high achievements in trade and civil liberty, have certain noteworthy gaps – especially in the field of eloquence – to be set against their impressive list of achievements in philosophy and science. By contrast with the English and Dutch, the French can boast of a remarkable, many-sided intellectual achievement; yet the culture of France is somewhat of a fragile hothouse affair laboring under the obstacle that the society supporting it lacks civil liberty and is commercially backward. By bringing to light the relative independence of the cultural and intellectual side of society from its socio-economic side, Hume's sociology of knowledge also points to the existence of certain dangers to civilization that the next generation of Scottish philosophers were to highlight: the great advances in wealth and civil liberty, far from insuring a corresponding advance in higher science and culture, could hinder it; consequently the material progress of the West does not automatically guarantee the maintenance of a level of philosophy and invention adequate to insure the intellectual and scientific progress without which society is likely to stagnate or founder.[20]

But these reservations about the possibility of progress constitute only the beginning of Hume's warning to contemporary society. Deploying a skeptical detachment toward established dogma, which rivals in its boldness that of Berkeley, Hume proceeded to bring out the limitations of the Hutchesonian doctrine of social optimism by a highly original critique of the social role of religion in which he presented it as far more equivocal, not to say sinister, force in civilization than either the freethink-

56

ers or the Hutchesonian moralists could conceive. A recurrent factor in social life, religion, for Hume, constitutes the unpredictable, questionable element that, by its sudden upsurges, can reduce material progress to nothing by stultifying the critical debate essential to the advance of civilization. At the same time, however, religion occasionally leaves some unpredictable good in its wake – as happened in England when the enthusiastic subjectivism of the Puritans, which had done so much to foment the civil wars, mellowed into a principle of civil and religious liberty. Thus, although the freethinkers might be right in seeing religion as an unverifiable or even a nonsensical metaphysic responsible for much harm, they are quite wrong in their idea that otherworldly beliefs are due to die out in the new age of scientific enlightenment. On the other hand, establishment writers like Hutcheson, although they estimate better the likelihood of the continuing importance of religion in the life of modern society, are equally wrong in their estimate that religious belief, if critically and rationally presented, can provide a stable basis for the ethics of a civilized society. On the contrary, religion is likely to remain a principle of perverse irrationalism: "Tis an observation suggested by all history that the religious spirit ... contains in it something of the supernatural and unaccountable and that, in its operations upon society effects correspond less to their known causes than in any other circumstance of government.'[21]

In such writings as the *Natural History of Religion* and the essay on miracles, Hume went on to give the reason why in his opinion religious phenomena were likely, for the foreseeable future, to defeat the calculations of the economists and the culture planners from which so much was hoped for. The fact of the matter was that, on the subject of religion, discussion between the learned and the vulgar does not lead to the same sort of common-sense consensus about standards that, in other fields of knowledge, were to serve as the support of civilization. Instead, it gives rise to irreconcilable disagreements of principle. Thus, in regard to the experimental sciences there can be some sort of *rapprochement* between the learned and the laity (not just the literate laity, but the masses). In the field of religion, on the other hand, concerned as it is with the transcendent, the teleological view of the experts is that the Divine is the imperceptible source of order and unity, whereas the vulgar (especially the masses) regard it as the imperceptible source of whatever is capricious, accidental, and irrational. In a series of essays[22] as entertaining as they are penetrating, Hume boldly expounds views of the disturbing divisive role of religion that seem to have been considerably substantiated during the last 300 years in the area most familiar to him, namely, the Presbyterian belt, which stretches from the Lowlands of Scotland up into the Highlands and across the Celtic Sea into the North of Ireland.

The third and deepest phase of Humean skepticism – the one where the unearthliness, as I have called it, of the Berkeleian influence asserts itself against the earthiness of Hutcheson – commenced as soon as the question arose for Hume as to whether it would not be possible for him to sketch a philosophy of progress that, reconciling the Hutchesonian common sense with the scientific reductiveness and shortcuts proposed by the free thinkers, would serve as a guide to what mankind would be capable of if freed from the irrational spirit that religion keeps alive. After all, Hume allowed the religious spirit, in spite of its firm hold on society, to be probably a contingent, intrusive, 'unnatural' element in mankind's equipment that it is possible to conceive as uprooted and abolished, at least in the distant future.[23] Why, then, should not Hume himself elaborate a blueprint for a complete system of enlightenment philosophy in the Baconian tradition? Gathering into one the valuable but fragmentary contributions found in the essays of English and Irish thinkers, this plan would bring together the learned and the vulgar in a fruitful program organized around the idea of experiment and observation, altogether freed from the irrationality of the suprasensible and supranatural. Indeed, so far as social philosophy was concerned, this common-sense goal had already been achieved by Hume himself, as the result of his criticizing Mandeville and Hutcheson in the light of one another. Why, then, should it not be possible to complete the system by extending it to cover the problem of our knowledge of nature, inherited from Descartes by way of Malebranche, Bayle, and Berkeley, not to mention Locke?

Hume was brought up in the education-minded polity of a Scotland in which, from 1690 to almost the end of the nineteenth century, the writing of academic textbooks of high quality was ranked among the greatest feats of literature. He was introduced to philosophy, moreover, by the works of living regents, the lectures of John Law of Edinburgh, and the fine edition of Pufendorf by Gershom Carmichael of Glasgow.

These scholars had played a prominent part in the controversial ambitions of preunion governments to restore the reputation of the country as a learned nation by sponsoring philosophical texts that might, at least so far as an academic introduction to the subject was concerned, be in some respects more satisfactory than those produced in other countries. Finally, Hume took as his mentor the professor of Ethics in Glasgow who, also brought up in the textbook tradition of Scotland, sought to write a compend capable of capturing the market from that of de Vries. Thus, Hume was ready on his own account, as he made clear in the essay on civil liberty, to admit the desirability of producing 'a standard book which we can transmit to posterity.' This would be a much better vehicle than those piecemeal monographs for making generally accessible as an instrument of enlightenment the first principles of the no-nonsense philosophy of experiment and observation that was England's great contribution to the modern world. In the event, however, the metaphysical difficulties Hume encountered in his prolonged struggle to produce such a book had the effect of convincing him that, however practicable the Baconian program might be from the standpoint of social philosophy, things stood quite differently in the even more fundamental field of intellectual philosophy – the philosophy of science. In the former it seemed to be plainly possible – at least if one kept out, by an abstraction, the irrationalities of religion – to evolve an experience-based philosophy that might serve both the vulgar and the learned, and through them the entire society, as a guide to social practice. By contrast, it was impossible in the latter complementary sphere – even if one kept out the religious element – to develop system-atically a theory of sense perception calculated to do justice both to the learned and the vulgar standpoints without at the same time finding oneself involved not merely in the metaphysical nonsense one meant to avoid, but, more seriously, in metaphysical nonsense so directly implicated in the experience under analysis as to be incapable of being in any way eliminated. Examining the implications of English empiricism in the light of the developments it had undergone when it came under the sharp scrutiny of the two sages of Dublin, Hume had found, in reference to the problem of the relation of knowledge to its sensory basis, that Hutcheson had been remarkably successful in re-establishing common sense about the intersensorial problem of sight and of touch against the fashionable reductivism that had formed the starting point for these strange Berkeleian speculations about the Divine visible language. But Hume also found that the Hutchesonian philosophy of common sense had proved powerless to shake Berkeley's even more unworldly speculations about our knowledge of the external world in which, by consistently pushing the simplifying positivist tendency to an extreme, which embarrassed its free-thinking proponents, he went on to demonstrate irrefutably the meaninglessness of our natural belief in body.

In the *Enquiry concerning Human Understanding* Hume speaks of the internal incoherence in the experimental philosophy that puts difficulties in the way of using it as an instrument of systematic enlightenment; namely, that the thesis about our knowledge of the external world expounded by Berkeley proves to be rationally founded to the point of irrefutability and yet incapable of carrying conviction, owing to its going against the 'authority,' as Kemp Smith acutely pointed out, of the Hutchesonian intuitionism. It is essential, I think, not only in the interests of Hume studies but even of the study of the classical Scottish philosophy in general, to understand that the contradiction spoken of by Hume is not between a rationally founded reduction of the *esse* of the body to its *percipi*, on the one hand, and a merely instinctive, nonrational refusal of this reduction on the other. Instead, the difficulty Hume brings to light is of a much subtler and deeper sort; *viz*, that in certain respects reason properly used is able to explain the grounding in experience of *some* of the paradoxical and seemingly transcendental aspects of the belief in body in accordance with the principles of classic common sense – the pooling of the sense files of sight and of touch – revived by Hutcheson. There is no need to have recourse to the reductions that led Berkeley to his doctrine of the Divine visible language. But beyond that point, in reference to more fundamental aspects of belief in body (those involved in its existence as independent of perception), reason deserts Hutchesonian common sense and supports or seems to support the reductive paradoxes of Berkeley. Illustrated by reference to the point put forward in the *Dublin Post-boy* in 1732,[24] which irritated Berkeley so much,[25] the basis of the opposition between Berkeley and Hutcheson that was to reveal to Hume the impasse at the heart of the experimentalist program was as follows. The interpersonal as well as the intersensorial comparisons make it possible for me to have ideas of the relative independence of body that would not have been available to me if I had but one sense or lacked the possibility of sympathetic communion with another person. However, the same principle of sympathetic comparison cannot, as Berkeley pointed out, clarify and justify the natural belief of bodies existing unobserved by any human being except by introducing the idea – totally without foundation in our ordinary experience as understood by Hutcheson – of the bodies' continued existence, when unperceived by us, as objects of experience to some superhuman being who is in a position to communicate to us about them.[26] What Hume learned from Berkeley was thus that the problem of belief in the independent existence of body is the obstacle that utterly baffles Hutcheson's otherwise remarkably promising program of converting the English experimental philosophy into a kind of a social philosophy of classical common sense.

But it was not only in reference to the question of the empirical basis of our belief in the external world's transcendence that Berkeley's intervention established, so far as Hume was concerned, the impossibility of the *rapprochement* that the revival of the ancient principles of common sense might hope to bring about between the contrasting sides of natural consciousness that were being highlighted in the struggle between the rationalists and the empiricists – on the one hand, the transcendental perspectives it seems to give rise to; on the other, the earthbound empirical foundations. In the eyes of Hume the impact on the learned world of Berkeley's *Analyst* played a great and probably decisive role in exposing the futility of the chief rival views of geometry. There was the simplifying modernist view that, drawing its inspiration from the Cartesian device of reducing continuous or geometric quantity to discreet or arithmetical quantity, starts with the technical notion of a point as a *minimum visible or tangibile* (an element incapable of being empirically isolated in principle by sophisticated procedures) and then goes on to give a definition, incomprehensible to the vulgar, of a geometrical line as composed of a finite number of juxtaposed points and of a plane as composed of a finite number of lines. On the other side was the ancient holistic view of geometry taken by Hutcheson's mathematics teachers at Glasgow (anti-Cartesian and pro-Greek in their mathematics), according to which a progressive series of comparisons, starting with ordinary three-dimensional bodies, elicits technical notions beyond the plain man's experience. By sensible abstraction this method discovers the germ of the Euclidean notion of lines and points in the familiar experience of the corners and the edges of things and then, by a revival of the method of exhaustion used by Archimedes and ancient geometers, ascends to the supersensible notion of a geometer's absolutely straight line or absolutely located point as entities capable of being approximated to without ever being reached. To the indignation of Scottish scientists Hume carried still further the skeptical critique of mathematics thus begun by Berkeley. He attacked with considerable severity the classical idea of the middle way in mathematics that, in a manner comparable of Hutcheson's work on the philosophy of society and of the sciences, Colin Maclaurin was contemporaneously engaged in developing as a counterblast to the *Analyst*. For Hume, the ancient method of starting with ordinary bodies in their concreteness and descending to their abstract aspects by 'a distinction of reason,' although it might work well enough at the level of sensible abstraction, entirely failed in its purpose at the subsequent stage of 'mathematical abstraction.' By appropriate comparisons of familiar objects such as roads it was possible to make sense, in a rough and ready way, of lines as possessing length without breadth; but the technical comparisons of the method of exhaustion, because they centered on the idea of approximating without ever reaching, were incapable of generating the quality of absoluteness required for mathematical accuracy. The modern method, however, based on the clear idea of the whole as nothing but the sum of separable parts – instead of the questionable idea of the whole as more than or different from the parts making it up – was up to a point more satisfactory logically. Properly understood, there was nothing absurd in principle about the idea of a line composed of a finite number of extensionless points, or *minima sensibilia*; yet, as Hume went on to point out, in the last analysis this reductivism was of no practical use in illuminating the basic ideas of Euclid since, as a matter of fact, *minima sensibilia* are incapable, either visibly or palpably, of being given in concrete isolation. Arguing in this way, that the Greek method, though perhaps practically useful in instruction and textbooks, is illogical, while the modern method, though logical, is unilluminating in practice, Hume is thus able to confront would-be revivers of the ancient philosophy of common sense with an embarrassing demonstration. However effective its comparative methods of the middle way are in clearing up

65

some of the modern problems (in particular those concerned with the interpersonal and the intersensorial), it nevertheless has nothing comparable to offer in reference to the most important problem thrown up in post-Renaissance time, namely, the elucidation of the very thing that had made the running in all the social and material advances – the method of uniting mathematics with experiment in the investigation of nature, as Hume's admirer Einstein recognised.

Viewed as a somewhat uneasy compromise between the Berkeleian paradoxes about the material world as the object of the exact sciences, on the one hand, and Hutcheson's social philosophy of common sense, on the other, the *Treatise of Human Nature*, despite Hume's attempts to give it a rounded appearance, hardly achieves the systematic character essential to the sort of 'standard-book' envisaged by him that could organize the piecemeal insights of his empiricist predecessors for 'transmission to posterity.' Moreover, Hume's difficulties in holding the two sides together were not resolved by the publication of the *Treatise*, and the more he pondered the problem the harder it seems to have become for him to uphold the claims of the vulgar consciousness against the philosophical doubts. Especially with the emergence of the contradictions about personal identity discussed in the appendix to *Treatise* III, Hume began to feel that the sceptical element was poised for a new thrust that would undermine the ordinary notions of conscience and self-valuation fundamental to the proper development of the Hutchesonian line in social philosophy and thus invade still more deeply whatever remained of systematism. Making the best of what was for him a bad situation Hume suddenly set aside his intellectual crisis by giving up the project of systematization in a grand manner, and by going back to the method of piecemeal exposition through essays, from which he had once hoped to escape. The result is the production of a sort of second philosophy, in which without either concealing the sceptical element or pushing it to extremes, he sought to cover the entire field of human nature from theology and theory of knowledge to economics and aesthetics in a markedly serial manner that does not emphasize the difficulties of finding interconnections.

However, Hume's repudiation of system did not prevent the other Scottish philosophers from taking up the problem where he left it. In course after course of lectures, professor after professor – Reid, Stewart, Brown, Hamilton, Ferrier, and Adam Smith, in some ways the greatest of them all – sought to overcome the tension between the common sense of Hutcheson and the paradoxes of Berkeley by producing a system that would harmonize the standpoint of the vulgar with the standpoint of the learned in a moderate philosophy of modern progress. Understood against the background of this century-long chain of thinkers, Sir James Mackintosh is surely quite right in presenting the two Irish philosophers, the opposition between whom is still visible in Ferrier's lectures in 1850, as having, by their co-operation awakened and kept alive the metaphysical genius of Scotland.[27]

Notes

1. *Dissertation ... Exhibiting a General View of the Progress of Ethical Philosophy, chiefly during the seventeenth and eighteenth centuries,* prefixed to the 7th ed. of the *Encyclopedia Britannica* (Edinburgh, 1830), s.v. 'Hutcheson,' pp. 348-49.

2. *The Works of George Berkeley Bishop of Cloyne,* ed. A. A. Luce and T. E. Jessop, 9 vols. (London, Thomas Nelson and Sons, 1948-57), 3: 44 (hereafter cited as *Works*).

3. Ibid., p. 117.

4. Ibid., p. 119.

5. *Francis Hutcheson: His Life, Teaching and Position in the History of Philosophy* (Cambridge, Cambridge University Press, 1900), p. 186, passim.

6. David Berman, 'Francis Hutcheson on Berkeley and the Molyneux Problem,' *Proceedings of the Royal Irish Academy,* 74: 259-65.

7. Each of whom presents a critique of Berkeley's *New Theory of Vision.*

8. *A Treatise of Human Nature,* ed. L. A. Selby-Bigge (Oxford, 1888), III, II, VI, p. 529 (hereafter cited as *Treatise*). Hume's position can be properly understood only if due weight is given to the discussion of the division of labour, found at the beginning of III, II, II.

9. *The Letters of David Hume,* ed. J. Y. T. Greig, 2 vols. (Oxford: Clarendon Press, 1932), I: 35, esp. p. 47 (Hereafter cited as *Letters*).

10. *Treatise,* III, II, II, pp. 498-501.

11. Ibid., p. 499.

12. See especially the connected quartet from Part I of the essays, 'Of Civil Liberty,' 'Of Eloquence,' and 'Of the Rise and Progress of the Arts and Sciences,' and 'Of Refinement in the Arts' in Part 2 (*The Philosophical Works,* ed. T. H. Green and T. H. Grose, 4 vols. [London, 1886], vol. 3 [hereafter cited as *Philosophical Works*]).

13. Ibid., p. 180. On the previous page Hume notes that poetry and eloquence may in their turn precede law.

14. Ibid., p. 303.

15. For the relationship between free and unfree societies see 'The Rise and Progress of the Arts and Sciences.' According to Hume, it is the free societies that, through their liberty of opinion make possible the inventiveness requisite to the rise of the arts and the sciences. The unfree societies, stifling inventiveness, develop chiefly by taking over techniques pioneered in the free societies; but, in compensation, they succeed in contributing to the movement of civilization certain qualities that are deficient in the free societies; for example, social discipline and polite deference.

16. *Philosophical Works,* 3: 301.

17. See *Treatise,* pp. 581-82.

18. This suppressed essay on essay writing is found in *Philosophical Works,* 4: 367-71.

19. *An Enquiry concerning Human Understanding,* ed. L. A. Selby-Bigge, 2nd ed. (Oxford, 1902), I, p. 10.

20. Laurence Bongie's study of the reception of Hume's *History of England* in France is illuminating on this point (*David Hume: Prophet of the Counter-revolution* [Oxford: Clarendon Press, 1965]).

21. *The History of England*, chap. 47, wherein James's visit to Scotland (1617) is described.

22. That is, *The Natural History of Religion*.

23. *Letters*, 1: 150-51.

24. 'Had we but one sense, we might be apt to conclude there were no objects at all without us ... but since the same object is the cause of ideas by different senses, thence we infer its existence' (Sept. 9 ed., in *Works*, 1: 277).

25. *Works*, 1: 251.

26. Ibid., 3: 147.

27. For example, see the problem posed in *Treatise*, I, II, IV.

Victor Cousin and the Scottish Philosophers

for Maxime Chastaing

In a philosophical point of view, Victor Cousin's relations with the Scottish philosophers – Hamilton and his circle in Edinburgh – are of more interest than one might expect, since the intellectual problem they were occupied with is a problem which is still very much alive in our own time – how the central tradition of Western philosophy inherited from Descartes can critically assimilate the classical philosophy of Germany from Kant through Fichte, Schelling, Hegel to Feuerbach. Originally, for Hamilton (born in 1788) and Cousin (born in 1792) the task of nineteenth-century philosophy was to return to the sanity of Descartes, by criticising the empiricist deviations on the part of Hume and Condillac from the Cartesian line, and to remake Cartesianism in the light of the Scottish philosophers, Hutcheson, Adam Smith and above all Thomas Reid. Suddenly, Cousin and Hamilton were faced by the revolution in philosophy which, as claimed by Heine in his article 'Germany' in the *Revue des Deux Mondes* of 1834, would, one day, destroy the intellectual inheritance of the West. *Deutschland bedroht die Welt* – at least in philosophy. Taking up the challenge first independently and then together, Cousin and Hamilton debated what to do.

The Frenchman was the first to speak out. In his philosophy of eclecticism, expounded in the famous course of 1828, Cousin argued that, for the renovation of Cartesianism, it isn't sufficient to restate it in the light of what M. Jean Laporte has called the reflective philosophy of the Scots. In addition, the psychology or phenomenology of Reid must be completed by being founded on an ontology or *a priori* metaphysics on the German plan. Hamilton, in his review of Cousin in 1829, disagreed. Cartesianism of the sort which Hamilton wanted, incorporating Reid's reflective psychology, is irreconcilable with the ontology of Schelling or of Hegel, and for its foundation in German philosophy can have recourse only to the Kantian critique of metaphysics.

The argument between Cousin and Hamilton developed into a kind of philosophical drama, not without romantic irony, when it became a triangle, as the result of the entry into the debate in 1842 of a Scottish philosopher of the younger generation, J. F. Ferrier (born 1808), who was personally one of Hamilton's greatest friends – they met almost every day – but who, in philosophy, was sympathetic to Cousin rather than to Hamilton. Believing like Cousin that Cartesianism, remade in the light of Scottish psychology, must find its ontological support from Schelling or Hegel, Ferrier in 1842 despatched to Cousin two articles[1] along with a friendly letter, with a view to forming an intellectual alliance which philosophically, but not personally, would be directed against Hamilton. Ferrier's advances were politely evaded by Cousin who, under Hamilton's influence was, by 1843, declaring himself more sympathetic to the prudent psychology of the Scots, and less sympathetic to the audacious ontology from beyond the Rhine. Ten years later, when there was a contest for the Chair for Moral Philosophy in Edinburgh, Ferrier renewed his plea to Cousin, writing a friendly letter which included a list of fifteen articles he had written by that time, while, simultaneously, Hamilton wrote also to Cousin requesting his support and assuring him of Ferrier's great admiration for his philosophy. However, once again, Cousin did not act. Finally, in 1856, when Ferrier, in the heat of the struggle over the relation of Church to State and of faith to reason in the Scottish constitutional problem, went to the extreme of rejecting the Scottish philosophy of Reid as a danger to Scotland and proposed to put in its place a new Scottish philosophy which would move from Cartesianism to German ontology by way of Adam Smith and of Berkeley, and not by way of Reid, Cousin abruptly turned against Ferrier, and in the great contest for the succession to Hamilton's Chair in 1856 gave his support not to Ferrier, but to Ferrier's opponent, Fraser, who was appointed largely as the result of Cousin's help.

As a Minister of Public Instruction, Cousin had succeeded in his plan of placing in Edinburgh a philosopher who could be depended upon to expound from the metropolitan chair a Scottish philosophy in the tradition of Hamilton, but more founded on an eclectic plan. But as a philosopher, Cousin's political victory had, without his knowing it, prepared the way for the ruin of his intellectual reputation, because Cousin's nominee to the Edinburgh Chair had far less sympathy and philosophical understanding for Cousin's neo-Cartesianism than had Ferrier, the defeated rival. By antagonising Ferrier, and banishing him to the obscurity of the tiny University of St Andrews, Cousin had silenced the voice which, more than any other in Europe, could have brought to light eloquently and clearly, the forgotten merits of the courses given by Cousin in the Paris of 1816, 1817 and 1828.

Cousin

Let us listen to the resounding voice of Victor Cousin as he disentangles the relation of Descartes to Reid on the one hand, and to Hegel or Schelling on the other. The indisputable contribution of Reid to philosophy is not so much that he 'broke the artificial bridge between the perceiving subject and the body perceived, by showing that we have a natural power of throwing ourselves, so to speak, from one side of the river to another.' Ferrier, in effect, is perhaps right when he says that Reid's doctrine about perception simply poses a problem which it does nothing to solve. But Ferrier, on the other hand is quite wrong when he goes on to claim that Reid never rationally proved one single fact, and that his philosophy of common sense always moves on the superficial plane of English empiricism. On the contrary, Cousin points out that the intellectual inspiration of Reid is, in the last analysis, Cartesian, not Baconian. For Reid, 'the infallibility of consciousness is the first of all truths.' This was the 'solid ground on which he took his stand in order to escape the floods of scepticism.' The important thing to note, Cousin continues, is that Reid in explaining in 1764 his method – the method of induction – invokes not the names of Bacon and of Newton then so much popularised by the Encyclopaedists, but the half-forgotten name of Descartes. Descartes, for Reid, is the true father of modern philosophy. 'Think what courage and sincerity, what firm conviction Reid must have

73

had to speak in this way in the midst of the eighteenth century to the scandal both of the empiricists and of the friends of the instinctivist philosophy of common sense.' (Victor Cousin *Philosophie écossaise,* Paris, 3rd ed., 1857, pp. 332, 311 (quoting Reid), 305, 312.)

But, after thus triumphantly repulsing the sceptic by invoking the Cartesian *cogito,* Reid unnecessarily exposes himself to a second sceptical attack, when continuing with his analysis of this incontestable fact of consciousness, he makes what Cousin calls 'an embarrassed comparison between conception and judgement.' (p. 368). To illustrate the contrasting but intimate relation between these two acts of mind, Reid appropriately enough considers the case where someone sees a man six feet high and conceives of a man sixty feet high, and where he judges that the first exists because he not only sees him, hears him, touches him, has reports about him from others, but at the same time judges the second does not exist because only he conceives him in the sense of finding his conception of a man of sixty feet high unsupported by any judgements of experience. Now in the ordinary state of life, in our mature consciousness we alternate in this way, Reid says, between entertaining a hypothesis or a conception about a state of affairs, and verifying our hypothesis by a judgement of experience. But, if so, then in regard to the dawn of consciousness, there arises, Reid argues, a problem as to the relative precedence to one another of conception and of judgement, similar to the classic problem of which comes first, the bird or the egg, or to the question, discussed by Descartes himself, in the eighth of the *Rules for the Direction of Mind,* as to how an art like that of carpentry can ever come into being because one cannot be a carpenter without a hammer and it requires a hammer to make a hammer. No doubt, as Descartes himself shows in the passage, it isn't so difficult to resolve the paradox about the hammer, but, the same Descartes, in speaking in the second Meditation about consciousness or thinking as including will, conception, affirmation, judgement etc., is sensible enough never to say which precedes which at the dawn of consciousness because – according to Reid – the dawn of consciousness is utterly hidden from us and it is impossible to know what it is like.

Cousin, for his part, was not impressed by Reid's criticism of Descartes. Reid, he says, is right in distinguishing between a mature state of consciousness and the dawn of consciousness, but he is clearly wrong in declaring that the latter raises an insoluble problem as to whether conception precedes judgement or judgement precedes conception. To say that conception might precede judgement at the dawn of consciousness is to say that we might begin by imagining a whole range of states of affairs before we had actually encountered examples of the states of affairs imagined, in previous judgements of experience which present them as existing. But, according to Cousin, Reid has thereby committed the absurdity of supposing that poetics, that is the theory of poetry, can precede the making of poetry or that the philosophy or the theory of common sense can precede the actual experience of our instinctive spontaneous common sense. By contrast, Descartes has been quite justified in his claim that consciousness carries within itself, from the beginning, a complex of affirmative judgements, not only about the existence of our consciousness but also about the occurrence of objects given to that consciousness as distinct from its experience. (pp. 368–75).

Properly understood, Descartes (Cousin affirms) can show us how to reconcile Reid and the Scottish philosophy with the ontological speculation of the German philosophers about the nature of consciousness at the moment of its dawn. Try to catch the rise of an experience in your mind, try to surprise yourself thinking without having intended or willed to think, and then you will find that to think is to affirm, that is, a judgement of existence and not mere conception in Reid's sense. Spontaneous and instinctive thought gives us, in virtue of its essential quality, first of all ourselves, the world, God, with their boundaries confusedly perceived, in a synthesis in which the clear and the obscure are mixed up together. Little by little reflexion and analysis bring their light into this initial and confusedly distinguished complex, and then everything becomes clear, definite and determinate for us. The self separates itself from the not-self, the self and the not-self, in their opposition and in their relation, give us the clear idea of the finite, and as the finite cannot be self-sufficient, it supposes and brings to us the infinite. As interpreted by Cousin, Descartes leads through Reid to Hegel, and indeed the leading ideas of both these philosophers are already in some sense contained in the *Meditations*. (Course of 1828, Seventh Lecture, opening pages).

The next question facing us is how Cousin, with some help from Fichte makes the Cartesian 'fact of consciousness' the foundation of our liberty, but we will postpone this topic until we come to Ferrier, who is sympathetic to the constructive side of Cousin. First, however, we will have to consider the sceptical Cartesianism which inspires the attack on Cousin by William Hamilton from the standpoint of the philosophy of common sense. In the event, Cousin's plan to use German metaphysics to bring new life to Cartesianism will be rehabilitated as the result of Ferrier's reply to Hamilton. (*Premiers Essais de Philosophie,* Paris, 1855, 3rd ed. pp. 244–5 – 1817 Course.)

Hamilton

To understand Hamilton's critique of Cousin, it is necessary to bear in mind that Hamilton seems to have accepted up to a point the Cartesian position as the proper starting point of philosophy. 'Consciousness,' said Hamilton 'is to the philosopher what the Bible is to the theologian.' ('Philosophy of perception' in *Edinburgh Review,* October 1830, pp. 158–207. Republished in *Discussions).* It is indubitable first, that I exist as a conscious being, second that in existing as a conscious being I am aware of existing in relation to certain objects of consciousness which are given to me as distinct from myself, in the sense of succeeding one another for my consciousness while I myself am fixed, and third, that the knowledge I have of these objects is partial and imperfect by comparison with the perfect unchallengeable knowledge I have of my own existence. So far, Hamilton agrees with Cousin, and the disagreement comes in reference to the final and so-to-speak Germanic element which Cousin finds in Descartes – the claim that my existence as an imperfect being implies in some way the existence of a perfect or infinite being, not myself. Hamilton draws attention to the ambiguity implied in this infinite/perfect juxtaposition. Are we dealing with infinite in the sense in which a circle might be said to be an endless line or in which a straight line prolonging itself in both directions at once might be said to be an endless line. We have no way of deciding between the rival interpretations as applied to the universe – whether it is absolute or infinite – either by experience or reason, and in any case Kant's antimonies would seem rationally to establish the paradoxical and absurd position that the mutually exclusive alternatives are both equally conceivable from a rational point of view.

But suppose Cousin comes up with the suggestion that perhaps Kant might be wrong or that we could settle the matter by introducing the Hegelian distinction between the true and the false infinite, the circle case being the former, the straight line the latter. Here Hamilton produces what he considers his trump card which, according to him, applies not merely in regard to the question of whether the world is a perfect whole or infinite, but also in regard to the question whether the bodily objects or shapes which we are conscious of as existing in distinction from myself exist independent of me and unobserved, or whether they have no existence when they are not present to my observation. For the matter of that, Hamilton continues, the very same sort of enigma arises in regard to the ancient puzzle as to whether we are free or determined – it seems impossible to establish conclusively or to refute either of these mutually exclusive alternatives. It will be time, Hamilton says, to take seriously evidence

Hegel offers in favour of the one kind of infinite as against the other when he made a better job of showing which of the alternatives reason recommends us to accept in the case of the external world or the problem of our freedom.

In the article on the philosophy of perception (1831) which Hamilton sent to Jouffroy and Royer-Collard as well as to Cousin, he clarifies and defends his claim in a careful discussion of Reid's relation to Hume's scepticism. Reid, says Hamilton, makes a good point against scepticism about the external world by drawing a distinction, similar to that in Ryle, between sensation and perception, the latter having as its proper objects the shapes and sizes of bodies other than one's own, the former consisting in vague feelings of interorganic strains and pains. But Reid is less successful against scepticism, when like so many philosophers from Berkeley to Hegel, he finds a key to the crux in the idea that the only serious illustrations of shape and size are optical illusions which are corrected by touch as a sort of illusion-free, reality-sense. Not only is touch beset with as many size and shape illusions as is sight, but far from being a reality-sense, our tactual encounters with an extra-organic body presents it to us only as something resisting our organic strivings which is vaguely space-occupying, but is unknown in its details. Finishing with a position more like Hume's than Reid's, Hamilton declares that in perception, we never get beyond the experiences of our own organism, in any of the sense fields – a paradox which his pupil Clerk Maxwell as well as his friend Ferrier were to find very stimulating.

Let us clarify the point by quoting a characteristic sentence from Hamilton to Cousin. 'I am, on the one hand, neither able to reject, nor to rise above, nor to overlook, nor, with Hegel, *überwinden,* the contradictions which are involved in every philosophy of the Absolute (the Principles of *Contradiction* and *Exclusi Medii* I cannot get rid of); and, on the other, I find that the great law, that the conceivable is always intermediate between two extremes, each equally incomprehensible, and yet contradictory of the other – affords a simpler solution than has yet been proposed of some of the most difficult and important problems of mental philosophy.' Hamilton's two extremes are illustrated by the contrast between the idealism which makes bodies mind-dependent, as Berkeley does, on the one hand, and the dualistic realism which makes matter exist independently of body in the strong sense of being altogether outside consciousness and represented in consciousness by an image, or again by the contrast between the extreme of an absolute freedom and the equal extreme of determinism. 'I know that this doctrine ... is a virtual scepticism in regard to the possibility of an ontology but I cannot help it.' Hamilton's middle way itself is supposed to find expression in the natural beliefs of a commonsense dualism which regards mind as having a face-to-face direct experience of the things it is perceiving, freedom as consisting of the perpetual struggle of the spirit to make the recalcitrant body obey it. (*Life of Hamilton,* John Veitch, p. 155).

Ferrier

Ferrier's contribution to the debate is best understood in the light of the manuscript course of 1849–50, about which he confessed a certain indebtedness to Victor Cousin in a letter to him of 1852. What is remarkable about this recently discovered Course is that it shows Ferrier to be as much an enthusiast for Descartes as was Cousin himself.[2] The object of what he says about Descartes is to correct the account of Cartesianism in Thomas Reid. 'Descartes' philosophy,' Ferrier says, 'has shared in the downfall which has overtaken his writings on physics, but it deserves a better fate. Never were works pregnant with more reality given to the world. By this I mean that they came hot and glowing from his own mind. His *Meditationes de prima philosophia* is the most wonderful and profound of all his productions, indeed of any of the productions of any philosopher who ever existed, in it was condensed the deepest and most laborious thinking of many years.'

An eloquent citation from Cousin prepares the way for Ferrier's claim that Descartes has still much to teach the modern world. 'I know not,' says Cousin 'what secret virtue it is which always brings Descartes into connection with reality. The force and vigour which animates him never exerts itself in vain. The school of Descartes may pass away but the movement which he animated will never cease to exist. Leibniz, Malebranche and Spinoza will serve to keep alive the merits of their master. Ignorance and envy may pretend that France is not congenial to philosophic genius, but to refute such an assertion she has only to mention the name of Descartes.'[4]

To understand what Descartes really stood for, according to Ferrier, we must introduce a certain qualification into Hamilton's otherwise stimulating view of Cartesianism. To explain Descartes, Hamilton had put forward the slogan 'Consciousness is to the philosopher what the Bible is to the theologian.' This principle, however, Ferrier says, is false and misleading if one takes the Cartesian consciousness in Hamilton's sense as affirming among its first principles the natural beliefs of Hume or of Reid, and is true only if one identifies its central principle with that of compulsory reason and nothing else. 'Reason was to Descartes in the reform of philosophy what the Bible was to reform in religion.'

Elucidating the meaning of this new version of the slogan, Ferrier differentiated himself from Hamilton and identified with Cousin in formulating Descartes' programme as being that the philosophy of mind must begin with empirical psychology and end in the metaphysics or ontology of the spirit, just as the philosophy of matter must begin with the experimental facts of science and end in a mathematical *a priori*. According to the Cartesian method 'all contingent facts of ordinary experience, internal or external, had to be tried by the test of reason. Such of them as the test succeeded in reducing from contingent to necessary truths were established as the absolute and philosophical truth. These, again, which the test could not reduce from contingent to necessary were marked off as possessing for the moment no absolute value in pure science, but they still possessed some value in proportion to their degree of probability.' Applied to the nature of mind, to the problem of consciousness, the doubt of Descartes therefore already shows us how to make the transition from the psychological and experimental facts to ontology which Cousin had sought in vain in studying Hegel and Schelling.

In applying this idea of Cartesian method to the relations of mind to matter, Ferrier starts from Victor Cousin's version of the primitive fact of experience as described by Descartes, that all self-knowledge presupposes in contrast to itself and as distinguishable but inseparable from itself, a certain experience of a variable not-self. 'When I perceive myself' Cousin says 'I distinguish myself from all that is not me, and in doing this I do two things, I affirm myself as existing, and I also affirm as existing what I distinguish myself from.' But there is, Cousin goes on, in this fact as given to experience, the complication that 'we do not distinguish ourselves in a precise manner from the world in relation to which we perceive ourselves.' (*Cours de 1828,* Paris, 2nd ed. pp. 153–4 and p. 168).

Starting from Cousin but going beyond him, Ferrier defines the Cartesian problem of the philosophy of mind by distinguishing Descartes' clarity from Descartes' confusion. On the subject of the experience of ourselves, Descartes reaches a clear, unchallengeable view because, in the *cogito* he brings to light a truth which is rational and necessary, but, by contrast, the second item mentioned – the relation of our self-knowledge to our experience of the things or objects of perception which are not ourselves – is never clarified by Descartes, because he doesn't succeed in discovering a necessary truth about the relation of the non-ego as given to us in our experience of it, and gets round the problem only by taking the circuitous and unsatisfactory route of invoking a rational faith in God. Like other philosophers, both before him and subsequent to him, Ferrier's first thought is to solve the problem by restating Descartes' view of matter in the light of

Bishop Berkeley. Berkeley's principle – the *esse* of body is *percipi* or to be perceived – will provide the necessary truth about the relation of our self-knowledge of the non-ego which will clear up the confusion left by Descartes by introducing rationality. Here, however, Hamilton, with Cousin's backing, objected strongly that Berkeley's position was philosophically unsatisfactory because he doesn't leave room for the commonsense idea of body as being given to us existing independently of our perception of it.

Ferrier takes up this problem in the two articles which he sent to Cousin, indicating to him that they offered, in relation to the Berkeleian-Cartesian problem of the relation of subject to object, a necessary clarification which was carried through in a genuinely Hegelian spirit but which, nevertheless, was original to Ferrier. At first sight, Ferrier's comment on his articles is puzzling, because they are quite unlike anything in Hegel. But the puzzle clears up when we understand that Ferrier's Hegel is not the German Hegel but rather Cousin's French version of Hegel. Interpreting the Hegelian doctrine of the world as a sort of organic unity constituted by identity in variety, Cousin had introduced the idea of two opposed but complementary laws. The one law, he says, that tending to divisibility to the infinite, to the atomisation of things, is certainly in the world, but how is it there? 'Only on condition of another law, that of universal attraction. The attraction is the return of variety to unity, just as the expansion is the movement of unity to variety. It is because the two laws are there in relation to one another that the world continues to exist.' (*Cours de 1828*, p. 150).

In the article sent to Cousin, the 'Crisis of Modern Speculation', Ferrier seeks to correct the Berkeleian subjectivity by showing that our perception of matter is governed by two contrasting but complementary laws similar to those of Cousin. The idealism of Berkeley can be consistently developed so as to avoid its one-sidedness. On the other hand, it can and must accept, as one law, the commonsense view of matter as existing independent of our perception of it. 'Unless we make some discrimination between our perceptions and outward objects, no consciousness or knowledge would be possible. This principle is one of the laws of thought, one of the first conditions of intelligence. But we allow it only a relative validity, it gives us only one half of the truth, and we shall show that if by one law of intelligence we constantly separate the subject and the object, by another law, we as constantly blend them into one.' (J. F. Ferrier *Lectures and Remains,* vol. 2, p. 270).

So far, all this is a mere application of Cousin, but the originality and power of Ferrier as a philosopher shows itself in the fact that, in restating Berkeley's position in terms of Cousin's two laws, he transports us suddenly from the world of Cousin to that of Merleau-Ponty and M. Sartre. The law of the blending of the subject and the object, of their indistinguishability, Ferrier says, consists in this, that if we isolate one avenue of sense – e.g. sight – from the other senses, as Berkeley tries to do in his new theory of vision, the objects of the sense thus isolated, i.e. the coloured shapes, at once lose their commonsense quality of being given to our perceptual consciousness as external to the bodily organs – the eyes, with which they are perceived. Our eyes are, in the ordinary sense, invisible to us, and when we separate visual experience from that of touch – as Berkeley does – we thereby cease to experience the visible shapes of things as external to our now invisible eyes in the sense of being at a measurable distance from them. We may see these visible shapes as in some other sense solid, as standing out in relief – Ferrier's critic Bailey already knew about the function of binocularity as exemplified in the stereoscope – but this fact does not prevent the depth of the visible things being invisible to us in another sense of our not being able to see them in relation to our unseen eyes. Merleau-Ponty saw this fact when he said that the depth-experience in vision was the most existential of all experiences.

The second law, the counter-law, according to Ferrier, comes into operation only when – as Berkeley suggests, we explore in a tactual experience, the relation of our eyes as palpable objects to the tactual aspects of the objects seen by them, and by this means discover, the requisite evidence for the externality and independence of the objects seen in relation to the organs of sight which make the seeing of them possible. Take away touch, and the evidence of visual externality, in the sense explained, disappears.

Berkeley, Ferrier says, understood these facts in relation to vision without however being able to analyse it, but what Berkeley failed to understand was that the two laws apply equally in the other sense-fields. Isolate our tactual experience of the solidity of a body not one's own from our visual knowledge of the relation of the tactual organ (whereby we feel it) to the visible aspects of the body felt, and at once we destroy our commonsense view of the solid body felt as being external to, and in contact with the tacual organ with which we feel it. 'We think' – says Ferrier – 'of hardness, solidity and resistance in one and the same thought with touch or some subjective effort,' the latter being given to us as indistinguishable and inseparable from the former. Ferrier has got hold of the same idea as Sartre was to put forward in *L'Être et le néant* when he said that 'my hand reveals to me the resistance of objects, their hardness and softness, but does not reveal itself.' (p. 366). For Ferrier, unlike Sartre, this result of the operation of the first law is corrected by the operation of the second law, which is that sight informs us of important aspects – not given in a tactual experience itself – of the relation between the organ of touch and the solid body felt. It is, for example, sight which enables us to know that the bodies whose shape and solidity we have felt continue to exist out of reach when we do not feel them. Ferrier finishes by giving his two laws a generalised form; no sense informs us of the existence of its organ and of the relation of that organ to its objects except by the intervention of another sense to which the former provides a reciprocal service. 'Sight pays back every fraction of its debt to its brother sense.' (J. F. Ferrier, *Lectures and Remains*, vol. 2, p. 367). The possibility of a vicious regress seems to be excluded by the mutual complementarity of the two senses, and thus by applying Cousin's two laws to perception, and by using them to generalise Berkeley's theory of vision into a general theory of experience, Ferrier begins to clear idealism from the accusation of subjectivism and to reconcile it with common sense.

What is very remarkable about Ferrier's use of the two laws is that in carrying through his speculation he applies to the letter the Cartesian method of clear and of confused ideas as he himself had explained it. First he starts from the relatively confused and complex fact of our consciousness through sight and touch of the bodies we perceive. Secondly by rigorous self-observation this confused and complex fact of sense-experience is clarified in an analysis which shows certain contingent facts composing it to be classifiable under a common head – that we do not see our organs of sight in the same sense as we see the shapes revealed by them and that we do not feel our organs of feeling in the same sense as we feel the solidity and shape of the things revealed by them. Finally, we carry the clarification to a new plane of distinct and rational ideas, by discovering that, in the system of apparently contingent facts revealed by self-observation, some are reducible to necessary truths or truths of reason whereas others are not so reducible. An example of the former would be apparently, the fact that our organs of vision cannot give themselves to our consciousness as one of the objects revealed by them, whereas an example of the latter, the contingent fact would be that the operation of our organ of sight, its capacity to show us a variety of things or nothing at all, is dependent on some activity going on in our brows and not on the behaviour of the lamp on the table.

Inspired by Cousin's idea that the Cartesian self-observation rests on a rational ontology similar to that of the Germans, Ferrier finally comes to sympathise with Descartes's vision that *a priori* facts both in regard to mind and matter 'are far more numerous than many people think.' (Descartes *Regulae ad directionem ingenii,* Regula III). Using hyperbolic language quite unlike that of Descartes himself to express the Cartesian dream, Ferrier predicts that one day necessary truths will come into their own. 'Ultimately they will blaze out as lucent as the stars; and like the stars, it will perhaps be found that they are numberless.' (*Institutes of Metaphysic,* p. 24).

Ferrier does not get far in fulfilling this programme, but he does succeed in pointing the way forward. Advancing beyond the limits of the analysis which sought to extend and to elucidate in terms of Cousin's two laws, the co-operation of sight and of touch in our perceptual knowledge of bodies not our own, Ferrier, in a couple of lectures in the 1849–50 Course, raises the more complicated and different question of how far our knowledge of ourselves can be decomposed into two parts, one which we learn in direct observation of ourselves, and another part which we can only learn indirectly from our experience of other people's communications, i.e. from our observation of their responses to us. In a luminous generalisation which is formulated only in a question set in a St. Andrews examination-paper of 1862, Ferrier points out that Adam Smith's theory of sympathy rests on a principle analogous to that which inspires Berkeley's theory of vision.

Just as Berkeley suggested that certain qualities of things which common sense considers as immediately given by vision, would be entirely removed from them, if the information given by touch about the relations between our organs of sight and these things as their objects was suppressed, so Adam Smith pointed out that certain qualities belonging to our bodies, which common sense believes to be given introspectively to us, would be entirely lost to us if there were a break in the communication between us and the other people in our neighbourhood. We know of the existence of these qualities of ourselves only because we learn from the spectators to see ourselves, as it were, with their eyes, because these qualities in ourselves cannot be observed by us directly and are only brought to our notice because the others draw our attention to them by looking at us and gesturing at us. 'Sympathy' said Ferrier, in the sense of learning to see ourselves as others see us 'seems to play the same role in the moral world as touch does in the physical world' (Lecture for 28th March 1850, University of Edinburgh manuscript). To illustrate this thesis, Ferrier cites the well-known passage in Adam Smith in which it is pointed out that, in this second-hand knowledge which we have of ourselves, the reactions of the spectators in reference to ourselves, as revealed in their countenances and behaviour, function as mirrors in the sense that they bring to our notice aspects of ourselves which are not directly observable by us, and which in the absence of other people to mirror them, would remain absolutely outside our ken. The expressiveness on our faces and in our gestures which, so to speak, register outwardly the way we feel about situations encountered are a case in point. We discover this characteristic expressiveness on the part of our bodies, not by looking at ourselves in mirrors or by using our hands to explore the changing contours of our countenance, but only by attending to the way the other people behave in regard to us. We don't get to know, for

90

example, whether our handshake is cold and reserved or full of warmth and friendliness, by shaking hands with ourselves, but only by shaking hands with others. Indeed, our bodily self-control in the matter of concealing or revealing our expressiveness is made possible only in keeping our eye on the others.

Ferrier doesn't systematically develop his doctrines on this point but a sentence or two of phenomenological description of the role of our observation of the other's reactions to us in self-knowledge not only shows where he is going, but also exhibits the sense in which Cousin's law and counter-law has a social application. Speaking of a direct experience of ourselves in abstraction from our indirect experience of ourselves via the mirroring by others, Ferrier says 'Feeling makes each individual man the centre of a system, round which all other men revolve as planets. Under its influence, man regards his interests and actions as of paramount importance, and the interests of others as of no importance at all; but sympathy, (i.e. our indirect knowledge of ourselves via our experience of other people's communications) counteracts the self-importance which feeling produces. It enables each man to view himself as standing at the circumference of things along with the others and not in the centre of the circle.' (27th March, 1850).

This distinction of Ferrier's coincides practically speaking with that drawn by M. Maxime Chastaing's article in the *Revue Philosophique* for 1954 – to which I owe so much – on 'Reid, la philosophie du sens commun et la connaissance de l'autrui'. M. Chastaing contrasts here 'the sentiment of which the Cartesians speak' with 'the social self-observation of which Adam

Smith speaks.' 'To the consciousness of my intimate experiences I oppose therefore the indirect and as it were pieced-together knowledge of self in which I know myself as another, which I have learned "in part" by means of the others and which I can get only by going back to my knowledge of the other person.' M. Chastaing opposes to one another what Ferrier as an admirer of Cousin's eclectism seeks to reconcile.

Yet a comparison of Ferrier's treatment of Adam Smith with Cousin's shows in a striking way how the latter's eclecticism differs from the former's *absolute or thorough-going presentationism* – the name which Ferrier (vol. 2, p. 404) wanted to give his philosophy, in order to draw attention to the fact that it was a self-presentationism in the sense regarding the problem of the observation of body as inseparable from the problem – neglected by so many empiricists – of the problem of self-observation or the observation of observation. (Vol. 2, pp. 245–251). Cousin admits a certain amount of truth in Adam Smith's point of view, in so far as there are certain situations in the moral life in which we as it were detach ourselves from ourselves and by communication with spectators, see ourselves from the outside with the eyes of others. (*La philosophie morale,* vol. 2, 1840, p. 150). But Cousin then dismisses Adam Smith's position on the ground of its applying to a part of our self-knowledge or moral self-observation and not to the whole. Ferrier, by contrast, is far more philosophical in the sense of seeking to generalise Adam Smith's viewpoint by showing it to be a different application of the principle on which Berkeley's theory of vision also rests – viz. the systematic difficulty or impossibility we have of observing certain essential aspects of ourselves and our bodily behaviour.

Nevertheless, Ferrier's analytic sharpness and originality must not be allowed to hide from us the extent and importance of his debt to Victor Cousin. It was from Cousin himself that Ferrier learned to apply the two laws to the problem of knowledge. Analysing with great intelligence the conditions of the problem, Cousin, 'in a solemn moment' had written: 'we know nothing except in ourselves and by ourselves; it is not ourselves who revolve about the external world; it is rather, the external world which revolves about ourselves; or if these two spheres have each movements peculiar and individual, but correlative to one another, we know this fact only because one of them teaches it to us: it is always from the former (namely ourselves) that we have to learn everything, above all the existence of the other, (namely the world) in its independent reality.' (*Fragments philosophiques* Tome 1, p. 327).

Ferrier echoes these words of Cousin when, in the quotation given above on the subject of Adam Smith, he speaks of ourselves as situated, from the point of view of our immediate experience in the centre of a planetary system, but, at the same time, as situated, from the point of view of our common sense, at the circumference of the system. Setting himself against the one-sidedness of a simplistic metaphysic, Cousin sought to bring back difficulty into philosophy. Ferrier will reap the benefit of this move. The genuinely philosophical problem would be to render consistent with one another two opinions which are apparently contradictory but which, nevertheless, can, in some fashion, be shown to be complementary.

But the indebtedness to Cousin emerges most strikingly in the way in which Ferrier, in his remarkable series of articles on the *Philosophy of Consciousness*, takes as the point of departure for his analysis and interpretation of the Cartesian *cogito*, Cousin's discussion of the subject, in the very part of *Fragments philosophiques* Tome 1, 1883 pp. 334–344 from which Ferrier got so many ideas.

'The intellectual procedure which reveals to us the fact of our personal existence,' as expounded by Cousin and further explored by Ferrier, brings us face to face with a problem which Cousin himself resolved by distinguishing between immediate abstraction and mediate abstraction. The distinction between the two simultaneous and inseparable facts which together constitute the *cogito* – my thought and my existence – is, according to Cousin, grasped only by an immediate abstraction in which one attends now to one aspect now to another – e.g. now to the object of our consciousness, now to our consciousness of the object i.e. now to the subjective side of an experience, i.e. to the experienc*ing*, now to the objective side of the same experience i.e. to the experienc*ed*, and *not* by a mediate abstraction i.e. the kind of abstraction which, by comparing several experiences of the same thing, makes it possible to differentiate the colour and the shape of a globe of white marble, to cite the example Hume uses (Treatise Bk. 1, section 7) or the straightness of a line from its length, to cite one of the examples Cousin himself uses (*Fragments philosophiques* 1838 Tome 1 pp. 347, 348), This distinction between mediate abstraction by comparison and immediate abstraction by shifts of attention is pushed to the limit by Ferrier, in his later work, with fatal consequences for his philosophy. Concentrating on immediate abstraction (the less well-founded of the two) to the neglect of the well-tried procedure of mediate abstraction, Ferrier, to the horror of Cousin, seeks to convert philosophy into a search for necessary truths, isolated from the experimental truths, treating the latter as belonging to the sphere of natural science – not that of philosophy.

By contrast, the theory put forward by Ferrier in the early part of his career, achieves its remarkable success because it relies on mediate abstraction in order to draw its well-grounded distinctions. Here, empirical distinctions, made by comparison, between the various inseparable aspects inherent in our perception of bodies – especially the distinction between the organs of sight and of touch on the one hand, and the experienced body which both senses have as the object of their perception on the other hand, provide, according to Ferrier, the preconditions, chronological as well as logical, for the supreme moment of self-discovery in which we first become aware of ourselves as the equals of the others, in the sense of being just as much entitled as they are to put forward our opinions and to have them listened to. According to Ferrier the comparison of sight and of touch which reveals to us the exteriority and the transcendence of the body perceived in relation to the experience we have of it is what makes possible the transformation which we experience from the state of *existence for others* i.e. existence in which our opinions are received ready-made from others into the state of *existence for oneself* i.e. existence in which we have established our title to be taken seriously by the others in the matter of the opinions we propound. The key to this achievement of intellectual maturity which Descartes sought to describe in his discussion of the *cogito* depends on the operation of a mediate abstraction which exhibits the ground of its distinctions and has nothing to do with the highly dubious procedure of the immediate abstraction which, it is claimed, reveals distinctions without being able to give any ground or reason for them.

Like Hume, Ferrier points to the new experiences of comparison which would enable us to make explicit the distinction which was originally implicit and hidden. Descartes's examination of consciousness is not, according to Ferrier, meant to prove his own existence, but to draw attention to two facts about his own existence which mark it off as very peculiar, compared with the existence of other sorts of things. First, Descartes is drawing attention to the fact, as he sees it, that, whereas consciousness, perceptual or otherwise, of mountains, of trees, etc:, doesn't infallibly imply the existence of the mountains and trees of which we are conscious, consciousness of one's own existence, by contrast, doesn't delude, and undeniably implies the existence of its object, namely oneself. 'Our thinking', Ferrier says, interpreting Descartes, 'does not make objects like mountains into realities. If they are realities, it is not so in consequence of our thoughts. But let us turn back from the universe and looking into ourselves, look at what is referred to by the use of the word "I", and here is our instance in which there is no distinction between the notion and reality.' The second fact which makes ourselves, or oneself, so peculiar or 'anomalous' as compared with these other things, in the way we are conscious of either, is, according to Descartes, as interpreted by Ferrier, that consciousness creates ourself, or oneself, in a way in which it does not create the mountains, the trees, and, for that matter, our own bodies, of which we are also conscious. Descartes, Ferrier allows, didn't say enough about this second peculiarity, but if asked about it, he would reply, or ought to have replied, something like this. 'Consciousness made me from being a *thing* to being a *self;* that is, it lifted me up from existing merely for others and taught me to exist also for myself'. The secret of Descartes's discussion of the *cogito* is that he implies, according to Ferrier, a social dimension to our experience which he does not make explicit. *(Lectures and Remains,* vol. 2, pp. 137-141).

Considered in itself, Ferrier's exposition of the two anomalous facts of consciousness is perhaps not very intelligible, but its meaning becomes tolerably clear when he goes on to restate it with the help of ideas derived from Adam Smith in his *Essay on the First Formation of Languages,* and also perhaps the Germans. Ferrier takes up the former's question as to what happens when a small child begins to refer to itself not in the third person 'Billy sits, Billy walks', but in the first person 'I sit, I walk'. What makes the difference, Ferrier says, is that whereas in the former case the child learns to refer to itself by the word 'Billy' in the same way as it learns to use properly the word 'table' to refer to the object meant – viz. by imitating the way it observes other people to use the two words – on the other hand, in the case of the transition to the first person pronoun as a means of self-reference, the child can't possibly learn the correct reference of the word 'I', as applied to itself by imitating the way the others use the word 'I'. The child can't be taught by the others to apply the first personal pronoun to itself in the way it *can* be taught by others to use the word 'Billy' in reference to itself, or the word 'table' in reference to the sort of thing it refers to. The child has to discover for itself, and can't learn from others, the rules governing the correct use of the first person and, presumably, the second person pronouns, both as they are used in application to itself and in application to others. According to Ferrier, the making of this discovery by the child is a momentous event in that it thereby establishes itself in its own eyes and in the eyes of the others as being the equal of these others, and so of being fully human. In the case of Descartes too, his discussion of our consciousness of our own existence has, in Ferrier's eyes, a similar significance from a moral point of view, and the outcome of the Cartesian discussions in the *Meditations* is to show the evidence behind our consciousness of the principle announced in the opening sentences of the *Discourse on Method* – viz. that good sense or reason is by nature equal in all men. Ferrier, like Chomsky in *Cartesian Linguistics,* is drawing attention to the social dimension of Descartes. *(Lectures and Remains,* vol. 2, pp 105-114 and pp. 252-254).

For Ferrier, the fundamental thing in Descartes is his description of the two stages requisite for our development to intellectual maturity We begin, as children, by believing what we are told without worrying whether any of it is doubtful, and we come of age intellectually only when becoming dissatisfied with the

98

ideas acquired through tradition and, at first not sure what to believe, we suddenly discover both the impossibility of doubting the existence of ourselves as thinking beings, and the necessity of directing our doubts beyond ourselves, at the ideas we find in the rest of the world, in case any of them can't establish their bona fides. This Cartesian position of questioning the existence of everything but one's own existence as an enquirer is taken over by Ferrier, and enriched by some judicious borrowing from the Germans. The initial move from existence for others to existence for self involves the emergence of a 'rebellious' (Ferrier's word) individualism in which, breaking with our original unquestioning identification with our families and milieu, we regard the other persons and things as satellites revolving around ourselves whom we regard as situated in the centre of things. The move from this individualistic stage of existence for self to the stage of existence as a socially responsible being is accomplished when, as the result of coming 'to see ourselves as other see us', we find ourselves out there with the others, revolving about an external world on which both we and they are dependent. Thus far Ferrier's position is very like that of Descartes, but in the sequel, this very important difference arises. Whereas for Descartes the age of reason, through cooperation of oneself with others on equal terms promises the possibility of man's mastery of nature, Ferrier and Cousin, on the other hand, regard nature not only as incapable of being mastered by man, but also as liable to frustrate human purposes, both social and individual, unless fortune is on their side. Religion, for Ferrier and Cousin, is man's way of reconciling himself with the dependent and precarious situation of our species.

Ferrier in his exposition of Descartes's discussion of the *cogito,* underpins it with various social ideas which he gets from the Germans as well as Adam Smith. Originally, as a baby, one exists for others, and one begins to exist for oneself only after having grasped the meaning of the word 'I'. Ferrier explicitly uses the word 'exist' here in the Heideggerian sense of a derivative from the Latin word 'extare', to stand out from. The root-idea here is, as is made plain in Ferrier's discussions of Berkeley and of Adam Smith, that one cannot in self-observation, observe oneself in one's bodily behaviour as distinct and separate from the things one is looking at and manipulating in the same way as in which one can observe other people as distinct and separate from the things which *they* are observed by us to be dealing with. (loc. cit. pp. 150–161, especially for Heidegger, p. 159). Ferrier, interestingly, in explaining the difficulty we have in distinguishing observationally ourselves from the bodies we are dealing with, has recourse to what one could call a Heideggerian etymology which was mentioned in the *Philosophy of Consciousness* as originally published in *Blackwood's Magazine* but which was erased by his Victorian editors of the *Lectures and Remains* 'The syllable *"no"* in the Greek word *noeo* (I perceive), I am,' Ferrier says, 'disposed to regard as the same as our negative word in English *no*. For *noeo* and all these words which imply knowledge, imply a discrimination made between the percipient being and the object he perceives' in the sense that the percipient being distinguishes itself from the object and denies mentally the object perceived to be oneself, the percipient being. As

100

Ferrier daringly put it in *Blackwood's* to *know* is to *no*. (Lecture 11, 27th November, 1849, Edinburgh University Manuscripts).

By this time, Ferrier has got far beyond Cousin, and yet his admiration for Cousin is well founded, since the inspiration of the remarkable *Philosophy of Consciousness* owes a great deal not merely to Cousin's discussion of Descartes in the 1816 Course of the *Premiers Essais,* but also to the limpidity and sensitivity with which Cousin in the course of 1828 brings to life the German ideas about the importance of the moment when self-consciousness begins. 'We do not begin by seeking ourselves for that would be to suppose that we are already in being, but one day at a certain hour, at a solemn instant in existence, without having sought ourselves, we find ourselves, we perceive ourselves.'

In all these works – the fifteen articles, the lecture course of 1850 and the book *The Institutes of Metaphysic* – which Ferrier by letter brought to Cousin's notice, there is no doubt nothing said or done about the problem which preoccupied so much both Cousin and Hamilton in the beginning as to the relation of the finite with the infinite, except, indeed, indirectly, in an interesting chapter on the nature of the will in the *Philosophy of Consciousness* in which Ferrier, using Cousin's notion of a law and a counter-law suggests that what keeps our world going is an antagonism between a law of assent whereby we are caught up in the causality of social pressures on the one hand, and a law of dissent on the other, whereby we assert our freedom by saying no to the social pressures. *(Lectures and Remains,* vol. 2, pp. 106–190). However, the passion caused by Cousin's refusal of support in 1856 seems to have stimulated Ferrier to take up the problem of the finite-infinite in a more definite and limited, and we may say professional way (in a modern sense). Raising the question first in 1856 itself in his pamphlet *Scottish Philosophy: the Old and the New*, as to whether Hamilton is justified in his defence of Kant's antinomies, Ferrier asserts quite brusquely, that in some sense which he doesn't properly explain, the thesis of the infinitude of space and time is right, or at least reasonable, whereas the thesis of their finitude is in some sense inconceivable. In an exploration of the question in the chapter on Heraclitus in his posthumously published 'Lectures on Greek Philosophy' in Volume 1 of the *Lectures and Remains*, Ferrier makes a quite new examination of the question in which, instead of arguing it out as he did in 1856 in the Kantian terms of the rational conceivability of the alternatives, concentrates its attention on the alternative ways of describing movement as perceived. Here Ferrier carefully works out a position which, without being Bergsonian in the exact sense of the term, may be described as a rational version of Bergsonism. The infinitist thesis applies to movement as we find it in our fundamental experience of its continuingness in which it has the apparently but not really inconsistent qualities – noted in Zeno's Flying Arrow – of the fact of the moving thing's being never in the same position for a single moment, but always so to speak in two positions at once. The finitist position on the other hand is exemplified in the way an observed movement – as of a falling body – has to be described by scientists before it can be measured by the use of the calculus or other devices. The body, in this finitist case is regarded in an artificial manner as occupying successive positions at successive instants. The principle which keeps the Universe in being, for Ferrier, is still exemplified best by the feature which he sees as fundamental to the infinitist position, the fact that it depends upon that antagonism between the workings of Cousin's two laws which in one form as applied to the physical universe keep the movement of things going according to rule by the attraction and counter-attraction of gravity, and which in the other case, of the world of human life keep things going by a different form of antagonism caused by the tension between the law of dissent or will, and the law of assent or causality.[3]

Understood merely in terms of the etiquette of professional philosophy, Cousin's remarkable decision to oppose Ferrier and to give his vote to Fraser in the 1856 contest can, up to a point, be explained by bringing into view a fact about Ferrier not discussed here – a certain disconcerting quality in his book *The Institutes of Metaphysic,* published in 1854 and again in 1856. In many ways a remarkable work to which the philosophy of the world is indebted for the introduction of the term 'epistemology' and which contains some irreplaceable chapters, the *Institutes* gives a very much more one-sided view of Ferrier's philosophy as a whole than the unpublished class-lectures of 1849-50 which I have followed here.

Like Kant in the *Grundlegung,* Ferrier eliminates the empirical or contingent element from positions already established so as to isolate the *logic* of his argument. First, there is a Berkeleian principle. Matter or body can't be thought of except as existing for

103

oneself as conscious of it. Second, there is a Platonic principle, newly introduced. One can't be conscious of (recognise) a particular thing without being conscious of it as resembling different particular things of the same sort, i.e. one can't be aware of the thing without being aware of it as a member of a class which isn't a unit class in Russell's sense, but which has to be thought of as having other members. Thirdly, there is a watered-down version of Adam Smith's principle, arrived at by putting together the Berkelean and Platonic principles. In being aware of matter as an object to the particular conscious self which is me, I have to be aware of this me as a member of a class of things – possessors of conscious selfhood – which is thought of as having other members, actual or possible, elsewhere. Fourthly and finally, the conclusion is drawn that, if all this is so, then I can't be aware of matter or body as an object to myself, without also thinking of it as an object to other selves who can be aware of its continuing existence, when my consciousness lapses.

By way of post-script, Ferrier casually slips in the caveat that the full aim of the argument – the refutation of subjective idealism or solipsism and the justification of objective idealism – cannot be achieved merely by the logic set forth above, but requires in addition an empirical analysis of the contingent part of our knowledge of one another which he speaks of as easily done.[5] But this way of setting the question is inexcusable, since it messes the sharp distinction between the logical version and the empirical version of my awareness of other selves. In the former, I am aware of myself as a member of the class of other conscious selves which may exist, whereas in the latter,

I am aware of myself only as aware of the other selves who *do* exist.

Provocatively presenting the *a priori* and the metaphysical as having nothing whatever to do with the contingent facts of reflective psychology, instead of deducing the former from the latter as had been done in the 1849–50 course and, in the process, obliterating the ultimate motive of his philosophy by keeping in the background, indeed almost concealing, the Cartesian sanity which was his real inspiration, this New Scottish Philosophy, as Ferrier called it in a polemical pamphlet, was understandably enough dismissed by Cousin as 'some importation of the bad metaphysics of a degenerate Germany' in *La philosophie Ecossaise* of 1857 which, in a kind of revenge for Ferrier's failure even to mention the name of Descartes in the book, omits the name of St Andrews, where Ferrier taught, from the list of the Scottish universities. What justifies, up to a point, Cousin's behaviour, is that in the *Institutes,* Ferrier presents the results of some of his early investigations in a form which suggests almost that he didn't fully realise the extent of his own achievement. In particular, Proposition 13 (pp. 310–320) utterly failed to do justice to the ideas about our knowledge of one another which he had developed in his lectures on Adam Smith and Sympathy, while, in the same way, Proposition 22 (pp. 384–401) in a similar way leaves out almost everything that is most vital in his analysis of perception as given in the five articles on the Berkeley-problem, two of which he had sent to Cousin. In addition, what particularly shocked the French philosophers was the immoderate, irresponsible tone – so different from the traditional circumspection associated in France with Scottish thought – in which Ferrier spoke of Reid as being 'outside his element in philosophy' and as being, compared with Hume, 'a whale in a field of clover'. 'When philosophers greet one another in the manner in which Mr Ferrier treats Reid' says Charles de Rémusat, in his notice of the book in the *Revue des Deux mondes* in April 1856, 'it is a day of diversion for the public, and one of the causes which has done most harm to the credit of the science.' No doubt, understood so to speak in Scottish and provincial terms, Ferrier's description of Reid as 'a whale in a field of clover' had a certain point in the sense that Ferrier wasn't denying Reid's great abilities as an intellectual man, but was saying that Reid's genius, as other people had said in Scotland and as might still be said, was exemplified to far greater advantage in his mathematical speculations about non-Euclidian geometry of the ninth section of the fifth chapter of the *Principles of the Human Mind* as well as in his altogether masterly essay on the history of Glasgow University, than in his philosophical works. However, whatever truth as there is in such a revaluation of Reid – and there certainly is some truth in it – it gets Reid and his achievement as Cousin saw it, completely out of proportion in that, in a provincialising way, it fails entirely to consider Reid's philosophy in comparison with the kind of philosophies that were being produced for university textbooks in other countries of the West. Judged by that standard Reid fares very well.

To assess properly the issue as between Ferrier and Cousin we must always remember that what we are discussing is not a quarrel over professional standards in the philosophy departments of the West, but a cultural-political crisis with a dimension in international politics as to whether the Scots could keep alive in the nineteenth century the compromise, initiated by the Union, of identifying politically with the English, but of maintaining a distinctive national identity before the world, in a cultural-spiritual sense, or whether, as has apparently subsequently happened in practice, they were to acquiesce in a new situation, not envisaged by the Union, in which they were to constitute a region of Britain like any other and not to continue to speak to the world with a distinctive voice exercising rights which were no doubt guaranteed to them by the reserve clauses of the act of Union but which were now beginning to have little meaning. Minister of Public Instruction in France for some years, who was himself 'a great friend to Scotland as well as to William Hamilton', Victor Cousin had no doubt of the value of keeping alive the Scottish intellectual presence as an independent entity in the West. 'My obligations to Scotland' – he wrote in his 1836 testimonial for Hamilton – 'have inspired me with a lively desire of seeing Scotland again represented in the Congress of European philosophers'. Hamilton too, though generally more cautious, made no concealment of his approval of Victor Cousin's plan of keeping alive the Scottish intellect on the international field, when in his Dedication of his edition of Reid in the late forties, he speaks of Victor Cousin 'as the statesman through whom Scotland has again been united intellectually to her old political ally' by the fact of 'the best results of Scottish philosophy' being adopted as 'the basis of academical instruction throughout the central nation of Europe.

Ferrier, too, as befitted one who was said to wear a sprig of thistle in his bonnet, was in his own way just as eager as Hamilton and Cousin to maintain the Scottish identity and in his notable paper on the Church and State crisis in Scotland, sought, with a combination of analytical profundity and warm patriotism to define a middle course which would resolve the dilemma of the country's 'perplexed constitution' in such a way as would restate and revitalise the old balance between secular interests of the Scots and their spiritual interests in a form suited to an age of reform and democracy. At the same time, however, as distinct from Hamilton and Cousin, Ferrier was not enthusiastic about an organised movement for keeping alive the tradition of Scottish philosophy. 'My philosophy' he said in defending himself against his critics 'is Scottish to the very core', in the sense of arising out of a critical working over of the ideas of Hume, Reid, Dugald Stewart, Thomas Brown, William Hamilton, Adam Smith, by comparison with Bishop Berkeley, Descartes, Victor Cousin, Malebranche and the German philosophers. But, Ferrier went on, 'philosophy is not traditionary'; its life depends upon personal genius and creativity, and the organisation of Scottish philosophy along a kind of party line which refuses to include in its ranks anybody but those who swear loyalty to the positions of Sir William Hamilton and Dr Reid is liable in the long run to be harmful. Cousin, on the other hand, in 1856 and 1857 in his Preface to *La philosophie Ecossaise* was emphatic that it was important not merely for Scotland itself, but for the sanity of the West, to hold together and prolong the tradition of Scottish philosophy in the form given to it by Reid. No wonder the tension between him and Ferrier turned out to be irreconcilable.

This essay is based on a contribution to the colloquium held in February 1982 at the Centre International d'Études Pédagogiques, Sèvres, and organised by the University of Edinburgh (J. Llewelyn) and the École Normale Supérieure (J. Derrida). The complete proceedings have been published by Presses de l'École Normale Supérieure as 'Victor Cousin: les idéologues et les Écossais'. The present text is a revised version of the text published in Edinburgh Review, Issue 74, 1986.

Notes

1. 'The Crisis in Modern Speculation' *Blackwood's Magazine* (1841) and 'Berkeley and Idealism' *Blackwood's Magazine* (1842).
2. Discovered by Arthur Thomson, it is in Edinburgh University Library, Dept. of Special Collections.
3. See also Edinburgh University Manuscripts Lecture 8, 21 November 1849.
4. From the publisher's advertisement for Cousin's edition of Descartes.
5. *Institutes of Metaphysic*, p. 310.

Adam Smith and Rousseau

1 Letter to the *Edinburgh Review*

If the Scots are to contribute creatively to the carrying on of English literature, without sacrificing their distinctive national inheritance of intellectuality, if the Scots are to avail themselves of the cultural opportunities opened out for their country by the Union they must avoid the policy recommended by the *Review*'s editors of taking their standards of literature from the London of Dr Johnson. Instead, the Scots, Smith claims, must look into the Paris of Voltaire and the Encyclopaedists where the values asserted by Bacon and Boyle, by Locke and Newton are far better understood than they are in the England of the post-Walpole era. In the first place, the France of the mid-eighteenth century was, according to Smith, far more appreciative than was the England of his time, of the imaginativeness and bold inventiveness which characterised the culture inherited from the England of Shakespeare and of Bacon. But in the second place, in taking up this great tradition of English culture which the English themselves had turned their backs on, the French, Adam Smith points out, have been developing it along the line congenial to Scottish talents and traditions in the sense that the Encyclopaedists of Paris have been adding to the ideas originally produced in England a systematic and philosophical foundation of a textbook sort which the English, even in their great days, had considered unworthy of their attention, and which even then they were content to let Scottish scholars provide for them. If the Scots were to follow the lead of the France of Diderot, Voltaire, Rousseau, D'Alembert etc. they will be in a position not only to make a distinctive contribution to English literature on the lines consonant with their country's ancient reputation as a learned nation but also win status for Scotland as the intellectual powerhouse of the English-speaking world.

Defending the paradox that Scotland's hopes of participating creatively in the culture of post-Union Britain are more likely to be realised by copying the uses made by the French of the classic literature of England rather than by imitating the Johnsonian generation's lack of interest in England's intellectual tasks, Smith, both in this *Letter* of 1756 and in his essay on the Formation of Language of 1781 made a point of emphasising the special value for the Scots of the part of contemporary French literature which was most thoroughly disapproved of by Dr Johnson, viz. Rousseau's Discourse on the *Origin of Inequality*. In the first place, if the Scots are to do justice to the social and moral problem of commercial society – i.e. the corrupting power of wealth – as posed in the last great work of English philosophy, viz. Mandeville's *Fable of the Bees*, they must go not to the pietistic criticisms of Mandeville made by the English themselves but to Jean-Jacques Rousseau who in his *Origin of Inequality* not only grasps what Mandeville was really driving at, but restates his point with a force and an eloquence worthy of Plato. But in the second place, as well as giving fresh life to Mandeville's critique of commercial society from a literary point of view, the more system-

111

atic approach of the French philosophy enables Rousseau to give the *Fable of the Bees* argument an intellectual dimension altogether lacking in the original, by making explicit the connection – apparently unnoticed among the English, though evident enough to the Scots – between the social problem as posed by Mandeville and the epistemological problem as posed by John Locke. Criticising Condillac's ultra-empiricist version of the Lockeian theory of language-learning in favour of the instinctivist or a priori position which we nowadays tend to associate with Chomsky or Wittgenstein, Rousseau, in the part of his work to which Smith calls particular attention, has challenged the optimism of the age, by arguing that, far from being kept in check by the spread of the Locke-inspired Enlightenment, the moral decline which notoriously menaces an advanced society organised around the egotistic principle of property, goes hand in hand with a failure in self-understanding which expresses itself in the individualism, the egocentricity of the theory of linguistic origins implied in Locke's empiricism. Whether or not Rousseau has gone too far in seeking to ground his social primitivism on a linguistic primitivism and in connecting the individualism of property with an epistemological individualism, is for Adam Smith a secondary issue. On the contrary, the important thing about Rousseau which makes him so valuable for the Scots is precisely the fact that he poses the question – hitherto overlooked in England, but beginning to attract the attention of the Scots – of the relations between the moral and the intellectual, between the 'ought' and the 'is'.

From Smith's standpoint, the quality which gave the

Origin of Inequality its profound relevance to his project of making Scotland the centre of an Enlightenment movement, which would revitalise England's intellectual tradition in the reflected light shed by its French admirers was that, as Smith himself implies, Rousseau, as the result of his Genevan background, comes close to the Presbyterian ideal of the unity of the vulgar consciousness with the learned consciousness, of philosophy with common sense, around which the Scots of David Hume's generation were striving to organise the inspired but unsystematic ideas inherited from the England of Bacon, Hobbes, Locke, Shaftesbury, Mandeville, not to mention Shakespeare and Milton. Significantly, as it seems to me, published in a review aimed at a purely Scottish audience, Smith's commendation of Rousseau's dedicatory remarks on 'the government of his country and the character of his countrymen' as 'an agreeable, animated, and, I believe, just panegyric' would seem to imply an actual acknowledgement on Smith's part of the value of Rousseau's philosophy to the Scots, in so far at least as it draws attention to the fact that 'the republican constitution' of Scotland's Geneva-modelled national church, which was the subject of so much retrospective pride among the Scots, contained within itself a set of cultural values which if properly realised, might enable Scotland to make a distinguished contribution to the secularised post-Union world of the future. In particular, the great image in which Rousseau sums up the character of his countrymen – the work-bench of his artisan father with the tools of his trade at one end and his Tacitus and his Grotius at the other – affirmed a value-system which,

113

however much it might have decayed in Switzerland or Holland, was still in Smith's opinion very much alive in Scotland, and with which Smith himself identifies when, in the Glasgow lectures he was giving at this period, he commends the literacy diffused among the peasants and ploughmen by the Parish school system in Scotland as giving them 'the benefits of religion not only in a pious sense, but as affording them subject of thought and speculation.' As spotlighted by Smith, the importance of Rousseau is that the dedication to the *Origin of Inequality* underwrites and endorses the Geneva-inherited principle of democratic intellectualism which the Scots already felt to be the proper vehicle for consolidating the spread of the Enlightenment and for showing the world how to check the corrupting power of wealth without too much prejudice to its increase and diffusion.

It was because Rousseau, alone among the French illuminists, was up to a point sympathetic to the peculiarly Presbyterian or post-Presbyterian ideal of the Enlightenment as the reconciliation of philosophy and the plain man, that Smith sat up and took notice when in the sequel he found that Rousseau's condemnation of the Encyclopaedist's project for spreading the light throughout the modern world didn't apply merely to the exclusive culture of the Parisian philosophes, but included also in its write-off this Calvinist idea of a broad-based humanism, the admiration for which had brought Smith and Rousseau together. 'The stimulating yet tantalising feature of the *Discourse on Inequality* for Smith was that Rousseau had first affirmed in his dedication the values inherited in common by Edinburgh and Geneva from the Refor-

114

mation as being appropriate only to a simpler and more antique type of civilisation, but had gone on to challenge their applicability to the new age of wealth and commerce, the characteristic problems of which had been brought out for Smith as well as for Rousseau in Mandeville's *Fable of the Bees*. The linguistic-epistemological excursus in the *Origin of Inequality*, although explicitly concerned with the Enlightenment in its reductive and Condillacian form, at the same time implicitly challenges the mother-idea of the Scottish Enlightenment as formulated by Smith himself, that the educational system evolved in the light of the second book of discipline – parochial schools where a peasant son might pick the smattering of Latin sufficient to enable him to proceed to the humanist colleges, could be adapted for the new civilisation of commerce and industry by a textbook reform which would keep alive a humanist breadth of vision in a society based on specialisation and science by substituting for Latin literature the Greek geometry developed by the Scottish mathematicians and by replacing the old metaphysics with a non-reductive version of the modern empiricist philosophy which wouldn't make nonsense of the transcendental values implicit in ordinary language. The problem set for Adam Smith by all this is that Rousseau, in spite of understanding sympathetically enough the cultural ideals animating the Scots, unsparingly attacks, both in the intellectual parts of the *Origin of Inequality* and in the essay on the *Origin of Language* which is its sequel, (both of them known to and cited from by Adam Smith) this pedagogical project of a consistent empiricism which would reconcile the transcendence and public reference of common sense with the inwardness of private experience, as being guilty of the same sort of contradiction as afflicts the sort of social philosophy which represents the private vices inherent in the property system of enrichment as compensated for by the public benefits resultant from it, on Mandeville's cynical analysis. From Adam Smith's point of view, as set forth in the *Letter to the Editors,* the challenge of Rousseau to the distinctive plan of a Scottish-based Enlightenment isn't so much the moral critique of the hypocrisies of advanced civilisation or the deschooling ideals of *Emile* as the attack on the idea of a moderate version of the empirically-based learning theory as being the key to a prosperous Enlightenment. Far from spreading light, the application of Locke's empiricism to education theory was, according to Rousseau liable to produce a perversion of culture and a stultification of civilisation.

However, Rousseau is not Adam Smith's sole concern in the part of the *Letter* concerned with moral philosophy. Without denying the value of the intellectualised restatement of Mandeville which constitutes the core of the *Origin of Inequality* and which was to be fully developed in the *Origin of Language,* Adam Smith nevertheless was leaving it an open question whether the socio-economic ideas of the English philosophers about material growth might not be reconcilable with the dualistic Genevan idea of the citizen as capable, like Rousseau's father, of functioning alternately on the manual and on the intellectual plane. The way forward for Scottish philosophy perhaps lay rather in checking and modifying the Rousseauistic critique of advanced civilisation in the light of

116

Levesque de Pouilly's popular and empiricistic restatement of Platonism in the Theory of Agreeable Sentiments which Smith commended in the Edinburgh Review *Letter* for the originality of its handling of its ideas borrowed from the English in large part. Published in Edinburgh ten years later (1766) in an English translation and provided with an introduction which draws attention to the qualities singled out for praise by Smith in his Letter, Pouilly's book doesn't claim to have any novelty except the systematisation of several ideas scattered in different authors. Its quality, the translator claims, is that it furnishes 'the key to the whole system of humanity and morality' in a philosophy which shows the pre-eminence of intellectual goods over physical goods without however entirely neglecting the latter. Plato is thus, according to Pouilly, perfectly justified in condemning the bodily pleasures as illusory by comparison with the intellectual pleasures because the former are all insatiable, like scratching a sore place, whereas the latter furnish the delights of endless discovery. On the other hand, however, Plato was wrong so far as in his republic he 'confined the vulgar to a profound ignorance' (p.226). In fact, what is really valuable in Plato may be 'established by the theory of sensation', that is by empiricism, and thus moral philosophy in its modern form is in reach of all. Calling for a sort of middle way between the reductivism of the French materialists on the one hand, and Rousseau's instinctivist primitivism on the other, Pouilly argues the case for a complex and mature type of empiricism which, as Smith was to do in his own philosophy, gives a due place to the neglected fact of sympathetic communication or social feeling – 'souls attract one another as a lodestone attracts iron'. Granted, that moral philosophy is concerned not with existing kingdoms but with the ideal perfection aimed at in politics, it at least gives us a measuring rod wherewith we can criticise our own age and society. Accepting, like Rousseau, Machiavelli's problem of the corrupting power of wealth, Pouilly refuses Rousseau's write-off of the modern empirisistic theory of human nature and society. Empiricism is for Pouilly a source of improved understanding and not a symptom of the disease of modern corruption it is supposed to cure. From Pouilly's point of view as commended by Adam Smith, Rousseau takes rank with Bayle as a 'Don Quixote'.

In juxtaposing in this way, Pouilly de Levesque side by side with Rousseau, Adam Smith is reminding his Scottish audience that the stimulating character of this cross-channel ferment over English ideas is due to the disappearance of the static consensus of Cartesianism and its replacement by a many-sided debate in the English manner, in which however, the relation of ethics to economics is discussed systematically in the light of first principles of knowledge and experience in a way which was foreign to the original discussions in the country of Locke. Restating in French terms the union of Platonism and common sense championed by Bishop Butler or Francis Hutchison, Pouilly makes up for any defects in the closeness of his analysis by a wide-ranging humanity which never forgets the connection of ethics with social history, with artistry, with physiology and modern science, with the culture of Greece, and the culture of India and the East. So too in a different and more profound way, Rousseau breaks

118

down the narrow particularism of English philosophy in his reworking of Mandeville and connects it up with the basis of human nature by drawing attention to questions of first principles which the English had been too apt to miss. '*What experiments would have to be made to discover the natural man and how are those experiments to be made in a state of society?*' Or again how is the theory of the origin of language and of knowledge to avoid the self-defeating and regressive procedure of the empiricists by which they are 'obliged to make man a philosopher before he is a man'. Just as Pouilly's popularised Platonism has for Adam Smith a genuine value so Rousseau has to be taken quite seriously when he speaks of himself as posing a problem which 'would not be unworthy of the Aristotles and Plinies of the present age'. What Smith hopes to bring home to the Scots is the value of the French contribution to the debate as having introduced a philosophical systemisation foreign to its English originators.

Contributed to a magazine which was managed by members of David Hume's circle but which – for reasons of controversies in the Scotland of the mid fifties as indicated in Mossner – never once mentioned Hume's name in its pages, Adam Smith's powerful Letter on the value of the French Encyclopaedists for the Scottish Enlightenment had, behind all the points it explicitly made, an ulterior purpose which would not be missed by its readers of giving their local hero and friend his due place as one of the 'Aristotles and Plinies' of the present age. What Smith as I read him was indirectly seeking to put over was that the problems of society and of epistemology so stimulatingly

119

explored by Rousseau and by Pouilly in their respective efforts to carry forward moral philosophy from the position where the English had left it, had already been examined more thoroughly and to more fruitful effect, in Scotland itself, in the *Treatise of Human Nature* and in the essays and Enquiries which followed it. Not only did the *Treatise* have two parts corresponding to the divisions noted by Adam Smith in the *Origin of Inequality,* on the one hand the description in Treatise I 'of the solitary state of man' which faces up much more fully and patiently than Rousseau to the logical difficulties of the egocentric standpoint built in to modern empiricism, and on the other hand, in Books II and III, a description 'of the first beginnings of gradual progress of social life' which, as in Rousseau, recognises and wrestles with the key notion of 'the vain desire of superiority' as the moving cause of human development, but, further, in *Treatise* III and in the *Essays*, Hume finally goes on to consider the possibility, rejected by Rousseau, that the empiricist scepticism of Book I and the possessive individualism of Book II might in principle be reconcilable with the ethical and intellectual values of the kind of society described by Pouilly which could fairly claim the loyalty and reconcile the interests, both of the 'learned' and of the 'vulgar'. Read between the lines, what Smith is implying is that in books which Dr Johnson might notoriously dismiss as lightweight, but which were being acclaimed by Montesquieu in regard to morals, and by Maupertuis in regard to science, as works of genius, David Hume was already revitalising the tradition of English-speaking philosophy by posing, somewhat earlier than Rousseau or Pouilly, the

Encyclopaedists' Enlightenment problem of the possibility of a synthesis between the intellectual, the aesthetic and the social ideas inherited from the English, that is to say, of how to reconcile Mandeville and Shaftesbury in the light of Locke. The value to the Scots of the French *philosophes* in general and of Rousseau in particular is that they remind post-Union Scotland of the importance of taking seriously the problems posed by Hume's intellectuality and of carrying forward the intellectual movement that he had done so much to consolidate. Looked at in the light of the work in France the fruitful contribution of Scotland to the culture of the world will consist in struggling with the problems common to Hume and to Rousseau, and not in submitting to the intellectual dictatorship of the sister-nation.

For Adam Smith, then, Rousseau doesn't serve merely as a foil to Hume, the function of which would be to show up the greatness of the latter. On the contrary, Rousseau's sceptical critique of the empiricist theory of language learning as well as his critical attack on private property and on what Hume called our 'esteem for the rich and great' serve to sharpen and deepen the problem posed by the *Treatise of Human Nature* obliging us to choose between mutually exclusive alternatives. *Either* we accept *Treatise* I's sceptical critique of modern empiricism as being Hume's major contribution rejecting Book II and III's cultural defence of commercial society in favour of Rousseau's condemnation of wealth and the arts connected with wealth *or* if we want to uphold against Rousseau the values of the science-based civilisation sketched in *Treatise* II and III we must face up to the formidable task of answering those sceptical parts of Book I which seem to more than endorse the Rousseauist doubts about the value of science. Bringing out for the benefit of an in-group the value of the philosophical tension between the *Treatise of Human Nature* on the one hand, and the *Origin of Inequality* on the other, Smith's Letter in the *Edinburgh Review* in 1756 draws attention to the remarkable quality of intellectual antithesis relating the Scot and the Swiss, which ten years later, working on commission from the former and in the face of the protests of the latter, Allan Ramsay will make explicit in his brilliantly matched pair of companion portraits – 'the Hume, direct, clear, luminous' and 'the Rousseau, shadowy and elusive'. Separated in our own time by an artistic bureaucracy which is unfortunately insensitive to the intellectual unity of the Scottish culture it exists to preserve, this incomparable pair of pictures, both in their contrast and their connectedness, body forth the central problem of the Scottish Enlightenment, as defined by implication in Adam Smith's early Letter and explicitly faced up to in his mature works.

2 Smith on Language

To get a comprehensive view of the principle around which Smith organised his *Considerations on the First Formation of Languages* (1761), we have to go to his comments (1763) on the manuscript programme by William Ward of York for a Treatise for rational grammar which was to appear in two volumes in 1765. Commending the quality of Ward's ideas, Smith at the same time is politely critical of their organising-principle as suffering from what he might have considered the English lack of systemisation. Drawing Ward's attention to the stimulating character of the French writing on the subject of language in the Encyclopaedia and particularly in the Abbé Girard's book *Les Vrais Principes de la Langue Française*, Smith expresses the opinion that a theory of language would best be organised around the principle of conjectural history, done in the French manner. The proper way to understand the origin of language is to see it arising on a developmental scheme in which the first words are so to speak complete sentences, and in which the various parts of speech such as we now have are evolved in a series of successive abstractions, in which explicit distinctions are drawn between the implicit aspects of their bent expressed in the original undivided utterance.

A 'Rational Grammar' of the kind Ward proposes, is, Smith believes, likely to provide not only the 'best system of Grammar', but the 'best system of Logic', provided its basis is a well thought out 'history of the natural progress of the human mind informing the most important abstractions upon which all reasoning depends.' From Smith's point of view the approach via speculative historiography is the important thing. 'If I was to treat of the same subject I should endeavour to begin with the consideration of verbs; these being in my apprehension the original parts of speech, first invented to express in one word a complete event; I should then have endeavoured to show how the subject was divided first from the attribute and afterwards how the object was distinguished from both, and in this manner I should have tried to investigate the origin

123

and use of all the different parts of speech and of all their different modifications, considered as necessary to express all the different qualifications and relations of any single event,' Qualifying this claim, Smith goes on to say that 'Ward may have excellent reasons' for following a different method, since, as Smith admits, the application of conjectural history to the problem of language raises great difficulties.

The nature of these difficulties referred to by Smith are made very clear by J-J. Rousseau in the passage in the *Origin of Inequality*, to which Smith refers us in his *First Formation of Languages*. Criticising the same sort of developmental theory of language as Smith has in mind – that in the beginning, single words function as whole sentences and that subsequently subjects and attributes, nouns and verbs are distinguished by an abstractive act of mind, Rousseau objects strongly to the central idea that the parts of speech developed as the result of a succession of abstractions from experience. In the first place, speaking with special reference to the version of the theory as developed by Condillac, Rousseau draws attention to the notorious unclarity, not to say illogicality, of the kind of philosophical analysis which sees in abstraction from experience the foundation and key to our grasp of the meaning of the various types of words. Discussing with great care the problem of the meaning of general terms, Rousseau sharply criticised the empiricist theory of the kind followed by Condillac, according to which we learn to apply correctly expressions like 'any bird' or 'any nut' by the sort of abstraction from experience which notes what individuals of the kinds mentioned have in common neglecting the points wherein they differ. How can an experience necessarily limited to *some* nuts enable us to single out the element they have in common with *all* nuts, in such a way as to enable us to apply the word 'nut' correctly to undiscovered specimens which may turn up, or even to unevolved types of nut which are mere possibilities, or again what about the special difficulty of the empirical theory of abstraction, that it turns on the puzzling and never very clearly explained notion of our being able to keep in view or attend to certain of a given thing's qualities while shutting out from view or being inattentive to other qualities of the thing which are given as empirically inseparable from the qualities we notice. Rousseau thus, working in his own way, rules out the simplistic kind of view which explains abstraction by an appeal to the 'wonderful faculty of inattention' mocked at by Gottlob Frege. From Rousseau's point of view Plato's view of our grasp of the meaning of general terms as being intellectually or instinctively based seems much sounder than Condillac's empiricism.

Condillac's theory of abstraction was, as Rousseau knew, not the only theory available. But from Rousseau's standpoint, the alternative theory of abstraction – such as that held by Adam Smith and Hume, which made abstraction depend on a complicated series of comparisons – was liable to the objection of failing to provide a key to the origin of language because the kind of abstraction involved – that explained by Hume in his discussion of the distinction of reason – would be far too difficult for primitives to achieve. The Humeian theory may illumine the type of abstraction made by scientists but just for that reason it is powerless to explain the birth of language among early men. Summing up its difficulty in a marvellous sentence, Rousseau tells us that 'the language of the first men is represented to us as the language of geometry, but we see that it was the language of poets'. Indeed, from Rousseau's point of view, it was not only impracticable but even logically impossible to explain the rise of language as achieved by some process analogous to mathematical abstraction, since the geometer is able to evolve his technical terms by abstraction only because there is already in existence for him a natural vocabulary, the rise of which must have been independent of abstraction. 'The invention of language did not proceed rationally, rather it was instinct that suggested to men the institution of sensate signs'.

The complications and subtleties of Adam Smith's theory of language clear up and become comprehensible as soon as we read it in the light in which he himself presented it – namely as a kind of critical response to difficulties started by Rousseau. Rousseau, according to Smith, is wrong in so far as he is sceptical of the theory of the parts of speech as developing by a complex succession of abstractions somewhat analogous to those employed by geometry, but Rousseau on the other hand is for Smith right in so far as he claims that it was instinct in the first place and not rational abstraction which gave rise to language. In the essay on the *First Formation of Languages*, Smith shows how to defend against Rousseau's charge of contradictoriness the paradoxical thesis that the complicated distinctions of an abstractive sort required for fixing the meaning of adjectives, prepositions, pronouns, number words as well as common nouns cannot be drawn except in a social group in which an instinctively based language already flourishes. According to Smith, the competing claims of instinct and of rational analysis to found language can be sorted out by a view of the developmental process which lets its speculation be guided by the actual facts of history, so far as they are available, and doesn't remain content with mere armchair guesswork. If we take the main historical direction of language-development to be the kind of transition – typical of the west – from an inflective language like Latin to the uninflected language found in Latin-derived tongues like French, we begin to get some good evidence that the terms whose meanings cannot be fixed without the analytic gymnastics objected to by Rousseau – words like 'of' denoting an abstract relation in general, or like 'I' or 'you', denoting the very abstract notion of personal identity – are distinctive of the speech of modern civilisations e.g. in English or German, or for that matter in modern Greek, and are less prominent in, and even in the last analysis, absent from diversions of the same languages current in ancient civilisation, whether in Greece or the German-speaking countries or the Latin ones. Analytic languages whose understanding depends on the operation of the rationalistic geometrical spirit pointed to by Rousseau, presuppose and arise out of synthetic languages in which the relation of speech to words is worked out in an intuitive or holistic or what Rousseau calls a poetic, way, without any need for the difficult abstractions.

Smith, however, is not yet finished with Rousseau's difficulties. If language started off instinctively with a pre-analytic stage, might not instinct, and not analysis, be responsible for the ramifications of its historical development? According to Rousseau as read by Smith in the light of Hume, the weakness of the theory which explains language development by appealing to abstraction from experience is not only revealed by the aforementioned difficulty – as old as Plato – of accounting for an understanding of general terms, which enables us to apply them to new cases, very unlike what has been previously experienced in the sort, but it is made more manifest in the apparent futility of modern philosophy's claim that this kind of 'sensible' abstraction, of which modern philosophy makes so much, can found and justify the dualistic distinctions of language between spirit and matter, inner and outer, which themselves transcend experience in the sense of having, as Rousseau says, 'no model in nature'. Dealing with this part of the difficulty not in the essay on the *First Formation of Languages* but in the posthumously published *Philosophical Essays* as well as in the metaphysical parts of the *Theory of Moral Sentiments*, Smith will, in effect, argue that, whereas the only theory of abstraction from experience which Rousseau seems to be properly acquainted with – viz. that of Condillac – is certainly incapable of elucidating our understanding of those terms which, like general words or the words expressing the mind matter dualism, in some sense refer us to what is beyond experience, the much more powerful and solidly based theory of abstraction which Hume struggles to develop in the *Treatise* – namely, the distinction of reason theory which shows us how, by a multiplication of appropriate comparisons, we can make explicit and in that sense bring within experience differentiations hitherto absent from experience, and incapable of appearing in it on account of their naturally being given to us as inseparable and simultaneous – provides us with the means of overcoming problems which to Rousseau appear insoluble. Up to a point, no doubt, Rousseau is quite justified in pointing out that the analytic spirit, which has been so much connected with the advance of modern science, carries within it the seeds of an obfuscating atomism and that the individualistic spirit, which has been the inspiration of the politics of modern freedom, confronts the thinking portion of mankind with what has been called the egocentric predicament. From Smith's point of view however these disadvantageous developments of the modern spirit can be compensated for and overcome by a theory of abstraction like Hume's which shows how it is possible for us to get beyond experience by comparing the views given by our various sense fields with one another, as well as by comparing our own personal experience of our relation to things as it is given directly to us in our own experience with such knowledge of our relationship to these same things as we can get indirectly by observing other people's responses to us. When looked at in relation to its epistemological grounding, Rousseau's critique of modern civilisation is for Smith not so much wrong as one-sided.

From Smith's point of view the modern philosophy of language, developed in the *histoire raisonnée* mode, is much better placed than Rousseau thinks to produce textbooks capable of enabling the plain man to participate intellectually in the march of science which characterizes the world of his own time and the immediate future. The ground-work of an analytic empiricism which will work out consistently and which is capable of further development has already been laid by Hume in the constructive parts of the *Treatise of Human Nature* – the theory of abstraction and space relations in Book I as well as the theory of sympathy and of society in Books II and III. No doubt Hume himself ends up in a sceptical tangle of the kind Rousseau points out, but as Smith sees it, the way to progress beyond Hume is to replace the sceptical passages in Book I on world perception and self perception by certain constructive contributions of Berkeley and of Condillac which have escaped notice owing to their faulty theory of abstraction. The result would be a restatement of analytic empiricism which, instead of contributing to the breakdown of the civilisation it is meant to carry forward and to the suppression of our instinctive and inherited understanding of life which Rousseau champions, would by becoming the basis of an improved logic and rhetoric adequate to modern civilisation carry forward the spirit of Enlightenment ending the artificiality of national differences. Taking it for granted that the intellectual emphasis peculiar to Scotland will fade away and be forgotten in proportion as the practical sense of the English and their political will begin to permeate Scottish post-Union life, Ferguson accepts the necessity of assimilation.

Admiring Rousseau as well as Smith, John Millar not only plays up the side of Smith which Ferguson plays down but even criticises Smith for not taking the intellectual difference between Scotland and England seriously enough. Smith is right according to Millar to insist that the alienation problem, as it has grown up in commercial England, can't possibly be properly faced by the English themselves until they develop an educational system somewhat similar to that already existing in Scotland, but he goes on to say that Smith entirely underestimates the difficulty of creating in England the conditions for modern education of the Scottish type, suitable for commercial society. Because of the peculiar form taken by the Reformation in Scotland, as well as some other factors which go still further back – one of them being the special relationship with the highly cultivated nation of France, the other the persistence into modern times of the semi-tribalised system which had disappeared elsewhere – the Scots have not only developed a taste for intellectual disputatiousness, especially on religious matters, but in addition they don't like to leave the final decision to the experts, but tend to rely on their own plain man's point of view. Hence, even among the farmhands and the operatives, education is valued, the modicum of money necessary to pay for schooling is not grudged and the schoolmaster is respected. This is very different from England where public education is not held in such high honour and where expert opinion tends to be taken as law.

The consequence is that the problem of education, which is for Smith the same in England as it is in Scotland, becomes different for Millar in the one country from what it is in the other. In England, it may be necessary to create the conditions for literature and education by roundabout governmental interventions – in particular a check on the excessive disparities of income – among the wealthy, by abolishing primogeniture, among the less well off by a certain amount of redistribution in pension schemes etc. – all done with a view to breaking down the barriers of communication between the various segments of the population, getting them to argue with one another, and through this inter-class argument getting them to see the value of public educational institutions. In Scotland, on the other hand, the problem is to prevent a living inheritance from weakening and decaying as the result of a Union in which the culture of the predominant partner tends inevitably by contagion to set standards for the whole, and in which the inherited bias is in favour of the poetic rather than the intellectual, in favour of practice as against theory, could, without intending it, put obstacles in the way of the carrying-on of the philosophical style of education developed by the Scots. Moreover, the situation of Scottish culture is still more embarrassed by the system of government by remote control which, like Fletcher and unlike some modern historians, Millar regards as the worst of all ways of ruling a country, the unhappy effects of which manifest themselves, in regard to Scottish philosophy, in the fact that the public honours of the United Kingdom go to James Beattie, whereas David Hume, 'by far the greatest philosopher and historian of the present age' as Adam Smith calls him, gets his recognition not from the rulers of Britain but from the rulers of France.

Millar's distinctive position emerges only after Smith died in 1790. No doubt as was the case with so many philosophical Scots in reference to their intellectual mentors – Smith himself in relation to Hume, Stewart to Reid, Brown to Stewart, and Ferrier to Hamilton – the pupil was reluctant to emphasise his difference from the teacher. Even so, in this attempt to

132

develop Smith's ideas for purposes for which Smith wouldn't approve – those of bringing them into service in the cause of the people – Millar remains somewhat uncertain as to where he is going, and modern commentators have noted two perhaps confused tendencies in his work which, I believe, can best be sorted out by recognising that one of them is a Foxite development of Smith aimed at liberalising the British or rather the English system, while the other is a development of Smith, the object of which is concerned less with the Union than with recognising the historical validity of the nationalisms of Ireland and of Scotland. The first finds expression in the anonymous *Letters to Crito* and *Letters to Sidney* (1795–96) in the first of which Millar attacks Pitt's policy of making war on France with a view to delaying the parliamentary reform in Britain, and the second of which, with due acknowledgement to the inspiration of Millar's ideas, (probably written by his nephew) expounds a kind of Smithian version of socialism which, implemented by the reformed parliament, would prepare the way for an educated democracy in Britain by a judicious redistribution of wealth (abolition of primogeniture, unemployment insurance etc.) calculated to bridge the class barriers and to stimulate public discussion between the few and the many about intellectual and general principles.

The second of Millar's lines finds expression in the remarkable essays on Scottish and on Irish history – posthumously published – which are quite different from anything in Smith in the sense that though consistently sympathetic with the French Revolution throughout the whole of its career, and unsympathetic to the rhetoric of his friend Burke, Millar nevertheless is what one could call Burkeian in his attitude to the national tradition which has developed in Scotland in the matter of intellectual consciousness. No doubt, the term 'Burkeian' is vague and arbitrary, but what it aims to convey is my impression that, for Millar, there has arisen in Scotland, owing to the peculiar combination of historical circumstances, – notably the Presbyterian form of the Reformation – a characteristic way of looking at life, expressing itself in a kind of distinctive tension between the intellectual principle and the popular principle, the standpoint of the laity and the standpoint of the experts, which has shown itself capable of providing illuminating comments on the world in reference to a state of affairs quite different from that of its own historical origins, and which on that account seems to Millar well worth preserving. In the event, the promised conclusion of the essay on Scottish history is not forthcoming, but the nationalist implications of Millar's thought, left unexplained by himself, are to some extent elucidated in the lives and careers of his pupils. In Ireland, some of the leaders of the '98 Rebellion in the north of Ireland certainly were ex-students of his who owned him as their master, and in Scotland the career of Thomas Muir points in a parallel direction. Friend of Hume and Smith philosophically and personally, Millar is ready to learn from Rousseau the importance of defending the democratic intellect by 'force of laws' if the 'force of things' fails to do it. Traditionalist as well as liberal, Millar thus prepares the way (through his Tory pupil David Hume junior) for the efforts of Scott, Inglis and Ferrier to keep alive Scotland's distinctive institutions – the Church, the law, education, and banking without gold.

The Mirror Theory:
Hume and Smith Against Derrida

Richard Rorty, towards the end of his *Philosophy and the Mirror of Nature* (p.371) suddenly becomes aware that Jacques Derrida has been defending the same thesis as himself. The upshot of the best modern philosophy – Wittgenstein, Heidegger, Dewey, – is that 'we must get the visual and particularly the mirroring metaphors out of our speech altogether'. 'Derrida's recent writings,' Rorty notes 'are meditations on how to avoid these metaphors'. (p.371).

Let us summarise the point Rorty and Derrida are making, by quoting from the blurb on the dust-jacket of the former's book. 'Since the 17th C., discussions of the mind and of knowledge have been dominated by the idea of representation. The mind is compared to a mirror which reflects reality, and knowledge is concerned with the accuracy of these reflections.' The lesson of twentieth-century discussion is that we must abandon the idea of knowledge as the discovery of the correspondence between thought or language and the world, and thereby give up the idea of philosophy as centring in a theory of representation. The future, Rorty goes on, belongs to 'a philosophy without mirrors' which will dissociate itself from Descartes' evidently unfulfillable programme of grounding or justifying science and knowledge in terms of these mirror metaphors.

The feature of Derrida and Rorty which interests me is that their argument in favour of their thesis is historical as well as systematic. According to Rorty, the thing which makes Thomas Reid an important thinker is that his attitude to the theory of ideas is a forerunner of the modern criticism of knowing as mirroring. The same sort of idea lies behind Derrida's long and careful studies of Rousseau and Condillac. Their pioneer efforts to set aside the Cartesian theory of mirrors and to make an empirically-based theory of language the starting point of philosophy are valuable, just because their social approach breaks with the mirror theory of knowledge.

What prompts me to enter into the discussion at this point is that both Rorty and Derrida seem to take up a one-sided attitude in their historical assessments. They refer to Reid, Condillac, and to Rousseau as critics of the mirror-theory without saying a word about a couple of contemporaries of this trio who differed sharply from them over the value of the mirror-idea – David Hume and especially Adam Smith. No doubt, Hume and Smith saw as clearly as Reid and the others the weakness of the mirror theory as used by Descartes, but, instead of giving it up, they sought to remedy it and give it fresh life. As the editors of the Glasgow edition of the *Theory of Moral Sentiments* remark – 'Reflection in Adam Smith is a live metaphor, for the thought process mirrors the judgment of a hypothetical observer. We suppose ourselves the spectators of our own behaviour and endeavour to imagine what effect it would, in this light, produce upon us.' 'This is the only looking-glass by which we can, in some measure, with the eyes of other people, scrutinise the propriety of our own conduct.' (3.1.5). Here we find the metaphor of light and the looking-glass which are ruled out by Derrida and by Rorty as self-evidently nonsense, and we find that, like Smith, Hume too has recourse to the same analogy when he is trying to clear up the relations of language and of consciousness. 'The minds of men are mirrors to one another', Hume says in his important chapter in the *Treatise* on our esteem for the rich and powerful, and, in the equally important chapter on abstraction, he points out that our ideas are illuminating – discover new facts to us – only in so far as they are '*accompanied by a reflection*, of which custom renders us insensible' (italics mine). What I want to do in this paper is to show how Smith helps us to understand the point of Hume's revival of the mirror metaphor – how it is useful for making sense of the problems of metaphysics. Hume and Smith thus hold to a view which is being denied by Rorty and Derrida, and the exposition of the contrast between their respective positions will, I hope, enable the chief point at issue to emerge very clearly.

Taken over from Hume by Smith, who expresses both in a more memorable way, this pair of *Treatise* slogans – 'men's minds are mirrors' and 'our ideas are accompanied by a kind of reflection' – restate the contrasting sides of the problem of knowledge, on the one hand knowledge as involved in our self-perception, and on the other hand, knowledge as involved in our perception of things. A mutual mirroring takes place as the result of which the perceived selves in the one way and the perceived things in the other way are able to throw light on one another, in the sense of making explicit and observable aspects of either which were hidden before. As used by Hume and Adam Smith in reference to the problem of self knowledge, this principle of mutual mirroring has to do with the fact that communication is established between a pair of human beings only insofar as each, in virtue of perceiving the other's reactions to himself, and of adjusting his behaviour so as to modify the other's perceptible reaction to it in a way that is appropriate, is made aware of the existence in himself – the way his feelings express themselves in his face and movements, the fact that he sometimes is asleep and unconscious – of certain of his qualities which would necessarily escape his notice in a solitary experience of himself, out of range of perceptual contact with anyone else. In perceiving something which no doubt stands out as a new object but which is otherwise undifferentiated, I can't distinguish one from another, and so make explicit to myself and to others its various qualities unless my perceptual survey makes it possible for me to compare this undifferentiated thing with some other undifferentiated bodies in regard to the resemblance relations. Just as with a solitary self-perception, when I am not in a position to observe other people's reactions to me, the mutual illumination can't take place which makes me aware of traits in myself incapable of being observed directly by me but brought home to me by my experience of the others in a reciprocal interchange in which I, in a similar way, serve as a mirror to them, so too when I am perceiving the one undifferentiated body by itself and when I am not in a position to compare it with other undifferentiated bodies, the mutual illumination can't take place which enables me to distinguish the various qualities in the body which weren't evident when it was first perceived. This latter case, the case of perceiving the undifferentiated body, is, however, complicated by the fact that, to effect a perceptual differentiation of the undifferentiated thing, it isn't enough to perceive other bodies which I can compare with it in respect of their resemblances and differences. For the implicit to become explicit the resemblances and differences noticed must be of a peculiar kind, and I couldn't begin to distinguish the colour from the shape in the globe of white marble if the other objects I perceived were exact replicas, or again were completely different – e.g. a globe of white marble followed by a sound followed by a pungent odour. According to Hume's view, it is necessary that there be at least three objects which present themselves as related by a system of partial resemblances AB/ AC/ EB – a white globe, a black globe, a white cube. In other words, the reflection can be illuminating only in the case where the ideas compared resemble one another in a certain respect according to the complicated pattern just stated.

Thus baldly stated, Hume's and Smith's principle of mirroring is no doubt too abstract to be clear, let alone carry conviction. However, once it has been tested in the fire of M. Derrida's sharp attack on the mirror principle, the point being made by Hume and Smith will emerge in sharp focus in the centre of the picture in the end. Whether or not the reader will be convinced by then, at least he will be put in a position to understand the problem.

* * *

In making this contrast between a comparison in which this mutual illumination occurs and the kind of comparison which leads to sterile and barren reflections in which we learn nothing, Hume, followed by Adam Smith, is seeking to throw some light on the nature of discovery or of getting new knowledge, in the sense of defining some of its conditions. 'Self-knowledge' is the reflection in which we achieve self-control in the sense of hiding our feelings as the result of discovering in regard to ourselves and our bodies the distinction of inner and outer, of what exists for ourselves in us and not for others, as opposed to the aspect of ourselves which exists for others and not for ourselves. It is thus conformable to our knowledge of 'foreign' bodies, i.e., of bodies external to us. To understand how self-knowledge can have moral effects, we have, Smith says, to modify considerably the mirror metaphor. The self-discovery which we make as the result of experiencing ourselves as stared at or gestured at by others is really more like what we find out about ourselves by looking at a painting of ourselves done by someone else than at a mere mirror reflection. Both the mirror and the painting show us physical aspects of our form and behaviour which aren't directly visible to us, but whereas the visage which faces us in the mirror – however uncouth or at odds with itself it may look – in some sort always chimes in with our present experience of ourselves whatever that may be – grave or happy – our visage, as shown to us by the painting, though it may seem formally similar to the other, exhibits us as having foreign and often repellent qualities which through familiarity we haven't noticed and which – as soon as we identify what we see as a picture of our behaviour – makes us uneasy with ourselves and turned in on ourselves in a process of trial and error aimed at controlling the aspects of our face and behaviour which is unobservable to us but observable by the others, so as to remove the quality which disturbed them. As the result of these blind experiments with ourselves we learn to control the outward expressions of our feelings in such a way as to render our conduct acceptable to society and to create a situation in which our feelings, as mirrored in others' conduct, become congenial to ourselves as well as to the others.

According to Smith, the first and chief rule of self-control, as learned in 'the great school of experience', is that if we wish to enjoy the approval of the others – and the desire for this is a basic human quality – we must hide from view all those parts of our outer agitations – observable to the others but not to us – which have their origins within our own bodies – in the pain of toothache, the pangs of greedy and gluttonous hunger, the torments of physical lust, however strong they may be. But though general experience recommends this role as an acceptable convention, a question arises of a speculative sort as to what we are to reply to some philosopher who asks for the justification of the role: to David Hume, for example, when he asks why we shouldn't prefer the destruction of the rest of the world to some hurt done to our little finger, or why we shouldn't let our outward behaviour express the pains which we inwardly feel rather than inhibit the expression of our private feelings in order to spare our competitors the pains or inward sufferings which they don't feel at all.

Smith's reply in effect concedes that in a two-person model of humanity, which would consist of myself and another person unknown to me previously with no particular connection with myself, with whom for some reason I find myself competing for some scarce good, that is to say, given an arrangement of society such as is envisaged in the 'master and slave' passages in Rousseau or Hegel (the former of which is actually translated by Smith in his letter to the editors of the *Edinburgh Review*), it might be difficult to provide Hume with a reason as to why I ought not to prefer the destruction of the other and perhaps his whole kind, to some hurt done to my little finger, given that in this two-person world created by my unexpected encounter with another stranger, perhaps of a different colour (Chinese, in Smith's case, *Theory of Moral Sentiments* p.136, Indian in Hume's, *Treatise* p.146), experience presents this other as a totally behaviouristic being, evidently devoid of feelings in himself, who, on that account, is not merely totally different from a centre of feeling like me, but who, by his unfeeling encroachments into my sphere, threatens to cause me the kind of painful experiences of which he himself is incapable. By contrast the world-model Smith uses is a three-person system, constructed on the principle that our two competitors, who find themselves devoid of any particular connection when they simply confine themselves to regarding one another, nevertheless do find themselves connected when, looking beyond one another, they each find themselves to be the common object to a kind of Sartrian 'third man', that is to say a spectator who, mirroring both in his countenance and gestures – that is, calling the attention of either to the fact that feelings each inwardly experiences, express themselves in outward bodily behaviour which are

142

beyond the experience of their subject, i.e. the man feeling them, but which are the principal object of experience to his competitor, in this way, gives each a looking-glass view of himself side by side with his opposite number, which brings home to them their common humanity by destroying their sense of apartness. Deploying this three-person scheme, Smith produces a very different picture of the human situation from that which we get in the two-person scheme of Hegel and of Rousseau. The master-slave scheme, for its part, finds no difficulty or paradox in Hume's question as to whether it isn't reasonable to prefer the destruction of the whole world to a hurt done to one's little finger, because, for Hegel and perhaps Rousseau, the self-creation of humanity and human society presupposes a ruthless struggle to the death between two parties, each of whom is aware of himself as a centre of feeling and drives but regards the other as a mere material object; the first stage in human development is that the victor in this struggle enslaves the other and turns him into a kind of tool and the second stage – the stage of the consolidation of human society – comes about through this tool's acquiescing in his servile situation when he discovers that as the result of his habitual ministrations the master becomes in a sense the slave of his slave, and the slave in a sense becomes the master of his master. By contrast, in Smith's system the challenge of Hume's question has to be met and overcome if we are to understand properly the foundations of the inter-relations between human beings. The sense of their common humanity is present from the start in the minds of the two competing parties because they always have among them, and are in communica-

143

tion with this third man, this neutral spectator, who not merely keeps awake among them an awareness of the necessity for standards of fair play, but who by his detached speculations – arguing, even in primitive times, as to whether or not there is a man in the moon – reminds the contestants that what differentiates the struggle for existence on the human plane from the struggle for existence among animals is that, among the former, the purely economic considerations are in some sense subordinated to or have to be reconciled with aesthetic considerations which have no meaning in the latter sphere, or in other words that the point of human society is not merely to 'live, but to live well', that the human passion for altering or at least being dissatisfied with their present social arrangements, has intellectual and artistic motives as well as purely material motives.

In a passage added in the second edition where Smith explicitly and consciously takes up Hume's question, he expounds his views about the necessary role of spectators by means of drawing an analogy of which Scottish philosophers are very fond – Hutcheson, Hume, Reid, Ferrier, as well as Smith – between the principle of sense-perception and the principle of moral perception. Suppose my sense of touch were in abeyance and I wasn't in a position to check my visual impression of things' sizes by going up and actually measuring them with manual measurements, it would be quite reasonable for me to believe – because of the lack, in the given situation, of contrary evidence – that the window which I stand beside and which is in the foreground of my field of vision is actually bigger than that which I see as it were framed by it when I look through it. It would be quite reasonable for me to believe – again because of the absence of contrary evidence – that some hurt or damage done to my own body which I was unable to observe properly because of my closeness to the event, and which I am acquainted with mainly by the severe pain caused me by it, is of far greater cosmic significance, that is, much more entitled to engross my concern, than the hurt done to the bodies of the Chinese by an earthquake, of whose nature and occurrence I can form a very accurate picture as the result of reports, but which after the initial shock of the news causes me no inconvenience and doesn't interfere with my sleep, on account of the absence from my experience of any evidence of the pain felt by its victims. But, Smith goes on, just as my comparative view of the respective sizes of the window and the mountain alter radically when the sense of touch returns, so too the reintroduction of the spectators into my experience of the world causes me to revise drastically my previous verdicts of the comparative importance of the hurt done to me and of the hurt done to the Chinese. Being now in the position to measure manually not merely the window by which I stand now but also the mountains which I can visit and measure with instruments from the foot, we now have satisfactory evidence that the latter are very much larger than is the former. So too, as the result of the mirror effect on me by the spectators who disclose to me my limitations of standpoint, I am now in a position to do what I couldn't do before, viz., to distance myself so to speak from my own situation and reconstruct, in imagination, a detailed picture of what happened to my body and how I reacted to the hurt as it might have been known to others who were eye-witnesses from a distance, or who had 'read of it in the news'. What I thereby achieve is an indirect view of my own predicament which enables me to know it in the same way as I knew indirectly the damage suffered by the Chinese, so that I can now compare and even in a sense measure the extent of the hurt done to me as known from the point of view of a neutral spectator, as well as the extent of the shock he would feel in coming to hear about it, against the extent of the hurt done to the Chinese and the amount of shock and inconvenience it would create if anybody heard of it as contemplated from the same detached standpoint. But having done this I have before me adequate evidence to convince me that I was not in the least justified in my first judgment, made without the help of the spectators, that the hurt done to me really mattered far more than the hurt done to the Chinese.

For Smith, the target of moral censure is thus the inconsiderateness of the agents who, engaged in some sort of competition or suffering some sort of hurt, make a clamour about this side of their life, the springs of their behaviour which are hidden from the spectators (i.e. the inwardly felt pains which, on that account, are immeasurable by objective standards) instead of confining their claims and limiting their complaints to the side of what they have done and suffered in competition of which they are aware indirectly as mirrored in the spectators' reactions, but which is directly and in the first instance accessible to the spectators. Here, however, Hume's question seems to recur in a new form: why should the agents be considerate to the spectators in this respect and why is it unreasonable for the agents to expatiate on their hidden woes and inobservable pains without regard to the spectators? Smith's answer (which is also I think substantially Hume's) depends on two considerations, the first of which is made very explicit by Smith. The first is that when the agent contemplates his actions and sufferings from the point of view of the spectator – something which he can't help doing because he wouldn't have learned language, how to talk about himself, without having done it – he is as horrified as the actual spectators about his own unfeeling egocentric conduct towards the others. The second consideration which is taken for granted by Smith, and isn't made explicit, is that the spectators aren't always spectators, that there is a regular rotation of roles, and that those who are now agents, involved in doing and suffering in the course of various transactions, expect the present spectators, when they in their turn as the result of the reversal of roles have become agents, to be considerate in regard to themselves in their new role as spectators, and to found their claims for justice on the parts of their behaviour which aren't private and which are brought to them as agents in the mirrors provided by the spectators. One may not like it, when it is one's own turn to be agent and to enter into competition, to find oneself pressured by the looks one sees directed at oneself by spectators into taking the same detached view of one's actions as they do, and into giving up all attempt to justify oneself by an appeal to one's private hidden pains, but at the same time one knows that one will get one's own back, so to speak, when the reversal of roles which makes *them* agent and *oneself* a spectator allows one to pressure them, by the looks on one's countenance, into taking the same kind of objective view of their behaviour as one does from one's spectatorial position and into abandoning their attempt to justify what they do by reference to their subjective sufferings.

Smith's point goes forward that one man's claim to deserve consideration from the spectators, superior to what they give to his rival, can't be made good by reference to imponderables like the hidden sufferings or secret extasies of either but only by reference to the side of the agents' behaviour which is directly accessible to the spectators, and which is indirectly accessible to the agents through their experience of the spectators' reactions to them. The only way that the claims of the one about what he has suffered etc. can be measured objectively against the counter claims of the other agent is that the respective behaviours which give rise to the claims and counter claims should be made comparable by being described in terms of the qualities which are accessible to and observable by the spectators and which the agents can learn about only indirectly by observing the spectators' reactions to them. Construed in the light of Smith's doctrine of the interplay between agents and spectators, the principle that equal amounts of toil and trouble deserve equal rewards makes no sense if the toil and troubles in question are taken as referring to the essentially immeasurable factor of privately felt but publicly inobservable pains, and makes sense only if they are taken to refer to something like measurable amounts (however the measurement may be carried through) of observable work which is performed by the agent, no doubt, but which the agent himself is less well placed

148

to observe than are the spectators.

Smith's position, as I understand it, is already implicit in Descartes' remark that we are not lodged in our bodies as a captain is in his ship. When his ship suffers sudden damage, the fact announces itself to the captain in the same sort of confused experience as announces to us the fact that our bodies have suffered some sudden serious damage. The difference between the captain's situation and mine expresses itself in the contrasting ways in which each of us clarifies the originally confused knowledge by getting a detailed diagnosis of the nature of the damage. The captain can get out of his ship and explore what has happened to it by means of careful observation, but I can't leave my body and for further knowledge have to rely on other people who communicate their observations to me and serve me as mirrors.

Edmund Husserl and 'the as yet, in its most important respect, unrecognised greatness of Hume.'

David Hume's quality of concealing under the deceptively placid, apparently limpid, surface of his philosophy, the passionate ratiocination of an insatiable thought that keeps on springing surprises and shocks, was already being commented upon, in his own time and his own country, as a fact all too liable to be overlooked, a century and a half before Edmund Husserl, writing in 1929 for a Continental audience, made his striking remark about Hume's real greatness as being still unrecognized in its most important aspect. It was very much this same paradox of the toughly cerebral core behind the bland façade that Adam Smith had in view, when, in the very emphatic language of his obituary letter, he warns us not to be put off by all that easy sociality and good nature into regarding Hume as, in A.E.Taylor's words, not a great philosopher but only a very clever man. 'That constant pleasantry', that 'gaiety of temper', which is 'so agreeable in society, but which is so often accompanied with frivolous and superficial qualities, was in him certainly attended with the most severe application, the most extensive learning, .[and] the greatest depth of thought'.[1] But the point both Adam Smith and Edmund Husserl are trying to put, that, if we want to get the most out of Hume, we must remember we are dealing with a man who to some extent hides his light, who, intellectually speaking, keeps much more in reserve and under the counter than he puts on public display – this point is perhaps most candidly and clearly expressed by his chief opponent Thomas Reid. One must always bear in mind, Reid was fond of telling his students, that in consolidating his literary reputation before the world 'Mr Hume appears to have forgot his metaphysics'. Anyone desirous of fathoming the full depth of what Hume has to teach us must go back behind the *Enquiries* to the difficult pages of the youthful work which its author disowned and which in consequence was being left unread.

However, it is not only that the leading figures of the Scottish Enlightenment coincided in this general way with Husserl in pointing out that the real nature of Hume's genius tended to be missed by his professed admirers, especially those of the empiricist camp. What is still more remarkable, Adam Smith, Thomas Reid and Edmund Husserl are also relatively close to one another in their more particular estimate that the greatness of Hume lay in the originality of his work in pin-pointing the intellectual weakness of our civilization and in thus opening the way to a new stage in the development of human culture. When, for instance, Adam Smith, in *The Wealth of Nations*, speaks of his friend as 'by far the most illustrious philosopher and historian of the present age',[2] he wasn't thinking merely of the point explicitly before his mind – Hume's originality in seeing, long before any one else, the intimate connection between the spread of the market economy on the one hand and the establishment of liberty under law on the other. He was also acknowledging his indebtedness to Hume for drawing

151

attention, as nobody else at the time was doing, to the deep and daunting problem of the relation of our advancing economies to the science on which they depend, both in respect of the considerable danger, discussed in Smith's *History of Astronomy*, of subordinating the speculative, unverifiable non-utilitarian side of science – the creative side (what Hume calls the imagination) – to the practical, bread-and-butter side, and also in respect of the equally real danger, highlighted in *The Wealth of Nations*, of the insidious growth, under a highly complex advanced civilisation, of an intellectual atomisation in which the learned and the conversable, as Hume calls them (that is to say, the polite part of society), get out of contact with one another, losing in the process the sobering sense of the common origin of their respective modes of culture in what Hume refers to as the animality of the vulgar.

Moreover, Adam Smith's estimate of Hume from the standpoint of ethical and social philosophy coincides very largely with those of Reid and Husserl from the stand-points of their respective epistemologies. As seen by Reid, the great achievement of the deep-wrought, sceptical arguments of *Treatise I* was to have brought into the open the fundamental flaw that had entered into the intellectual structure of our civilization at the time of its birth in Greece and that had not been exposed and eliminated by the great Cartesian reform – namely, an excess of technical bias, which had, from the first, cut philosophy off from the plain man by divorcing it from the realist standpoint of common sense. Exposing for the first time the real nature of this built-in contradiction, the author of the *Treatise*, amid all the confusions of his impressions and ideas and without exactly knowing what he was doing, had prepared the way for what Reid called the 'third age of humanity' – the Age of Common Sense which, advancing beyond the previous two ages, the Aristotelian and the Cartesian, would at last bring to an end the fatal division between the learned and the vulgar, by bringing to light a new *a priori* of first principles less simplified than the Cartesian, less complex and animistic than the Aristotelian. Sharing Reid's epistemological standpoint but more favourable than he to the constructive side of *Treatise I*, Husserl seems to be claiming, in a manner very similar to Reid's, that Hume's significance as a keythinker lies in his showing the way to our bringing to a triumphant fulfilment the programme for a pre-suppositionless philosophy, which had been inaugurated, but not carried through, by Descartes at the beginning of the scientific era. Properly developed along phenomenological lines, Hume's much-questioned impressions and ideas provided a clue for evolving a new sort of material a priori capable of closing the gap, so disastrous for Descartes' dream, between the teachings of nature on the one hand and the light of nature on the other. Thus, just as for Reid, the metaphysical passages in *Treatise I*, which Hume preferred to forget about in the *Enquiries*, or, for Smith, the analysis of the relations of the learned professions with polite society, which Hume was later to exclude from his essays,[3] possessed the special significance of opening the way for a philosophy capable of coping with the modern version of the intellectual atomisation, which had been in part responsible for the ruin of classical civilization, so in a somewhat similar way for Husserl, 'the as yet, in its most important respect, unrecognized greatness of Hume' would seem to have consisted in Hume's vital role in discovering an intellectual method that would bring into being the critical inwardness requisite to offset the over-extrovert science of our time without stifling its great qualities.

If we are to understand aright the general sense of Husserl's high claims as to the hidden depths of the Humean philosophy, we must, I believe, take him to be re-asserting in twentieth-century terms very much the same thing as Reid was trying to make explicit for his scholarly auditors and as Adam Smith was trying to put over for the serious public at large: that Hume's rather sceptical attitude to the Baconian schemes for modern civilization, far from simply spotlighting the merely practical difficulties of realizing the radical version of the scientific dream, in reality is concerned with bringing to light certain fundamental difficulties of principle, epistemological as well as ethical, which if not removed would seem to make nonsense of the whole experimentalist programme of modern civilization. Looking back to Hume from the standpoint of our century, Husserl thus, in some measure, recaptures insights originally won by Adam Smith and Reid and lost again by Bentham and the Mills – namely, that, while David Hume certainly accepts as his starting point the post-renaissance scheme for a science-based renewal of civilization in which material advance was to proceed side by side with intellectual advance, he differed very sharply from the other standard-bearers of the Enlightenment, French as well as English, in respect of the question of the relative importance of the theoretical elements in the programme as opposed to the practical, refusing to regard the theoretical problem as a simple and secondary one that already, in principle, had been solved, and uncovering the scandal of the basic epistemological contradictions that made nonsense of all the high claims about the Age of Reason. Thus, whereas adherents to the experimental philosophy, whether the 'philosophers' and associationists of the eighteenth century or the logical positivists and linguistic philosophers of the present age, tend to be of the opinion that the application of science for the practical end of providing a sufficient quantity of goods and shelter for all was modern civilization's primary practical task, by comparison with which the merely theoretical issues of founding science on experience or diffusing its spirit through the society were of very secondary importance, presenting no great difficulties of principle and safely left to solve themselves by *laissez-faire*, the uniqueness of David Hume, glimpsed by Husserl as well as by Reid and Adam Smith, consisted in his seeing that the purely intellectual side of the problems of civilization was not only as difficult as the practical side but even in some sense constituted the key to the latter.

It was only at the very end of Husserl's career that he gave to the world *The Crisis of the European Sciences*, which, far more than any of his other books, begins to make explicit his developing affinity with Reid and the Scottish philosophers, not only in respect of its drawing attention, as they do, to the hidden significance of the overlooked paradoxes of the *Treatise* for the future of humanity, but even in respect of its locating the roots of Europe's scientific crisis precisely where the

Scottish school had located them – namely, in the reductive, atomising procedures fatefully introduced by Descartes' arithmetization of geometry. Already, some fifty or sixty years before the appearance of the *Krisis* in 1936, certain traces of common-ground with the classical philosophy of Scotland, as developed in and through the tension between David Hume and the Scottish geometers, would seem to have been present at the very start of what was to become the phenomenological movement – in Franz Brentano's lectures on the *Treatise of Human Nature*, which Husserl would have heard in his student days. Thus in the very decade – the seventies of the last century when, amid the final decadence and disruption of the presbyterian polity, the intellectual pre-eminence of Edinburgh as a centre of philosophy and science was overtaken and overthrown by the rising prestige of the cultural contribution of South Britain, some of the leading ideas of the Scottish school – especially those centring in its tradition of Hume-scholarship but also some of those connected with its tradition of a holistic mathematics as reviewed by Hamilton's pupil Clerk Maxwell in the Preface to his epoch-making *Treatise on Magnetism and Electricity* (1873) migrated to the Continent to find a congenial home as a provocative subject of intellectual discussion, in an Austrian Empire, which, amid a growing decadence and disruptiveness of a somewhat more spectacular sort than our Scottish species, was in the process of becoming the new hot-bed of Western ideas.

Indeed, as far as central Europe was concerned, the widely influential and forceful books produced in the England of those years with the aim of finally extirpat-

156

ing the Scottish pretensions to philosophical eminence – J. S. Mill's, *An Examination of Sir William Hamilton's Philosophy* (1865) and T.H.Green's Preface to the *Treatise of Human Nature* (1874) – had the unintended effect of awakening in Prague and Vienna a certain interest in the very authors whom their polemics had intended to discredit, since in the tortuous intellectual milieu of Mittel-Europa, the metaphysical doubts and difficulties expounded by Hume and by Hamilton, the last of the Reid school, in some respects seemed to have about them a deeper ring of reality than the earnest expositions of the British liberal ideal. Accordingly in the discussions and criticisms of the English-language philosophy on which Husserl was brought up, the key figures, one might say, were Hamilton and Hume, the men who, in the words of the former, were intent on re-installing on his throne the good god Difficulty, rather than the ethical-minded men-of-affairs like Mill and Green who, it appears, were always right on all the Trade Union issues of the day but by whom the metaphysical problem as such had been relegated to a very secondary place. Faced with the enthusiastic out-pouring of this pair of high-minded polemists, the Austrians fastened with relief and curiosity on the problem of abstraction in Scottish philosophy as the one and only feature of it about which Mill and Green had a good word to say – the former singling out Hamilton's theory of abstraction by shifts of attention as the only decent thing in his books, the latter treating Hume's distinctions of reason theory as the only intelligible item in the whole *Treatise*. Stimulated by the novelty of what they found in Hume and Hamilton on the subject, the German-

157

speaking philosophers of the Brentano circle concentrated on it to the neglect of everything else in Mill and in Green, treating the Scottish tension over the abstraction problem as the most significant item in the whole tradition of British Empiricism.

Husserl, a relatively slow developer, seems to have begun, like others of the Brentano school, especially Meinong in his 1877 *Hume-Studies* I, by taking Hamilton's side against Hume in the controversy over the nature of abstraction, and the intellectually creative period of Husserl's life did not, one might say, get properly going until, just about the beginning of the present century, he reacted against the Hamiltonian ideas sponsored by Meinong, and switched to the Humean side, digging for stimulus in the unread pages of the *Treatise* and encouraging his pupils to do the same. With that, things suddenly began to happen, and from then on his thought began to move forward in a curiously double-sided progress, alternately historical and systematic, by turns backward-looking and forward-looking, in which each creative contribution to the twentieth-century problem of analysis was accompanied, consolidated and perhaps sometimes sparked off, by fresh discoveries in the hidden parts of Hume's text, discoveries which sought to get behind the stereotype interpretations handed down from Hamilton and the final scholastic period of the Scottish school. In the first place, the emergence of the characteristically Husserlian theory of perception in and through the variations of perspective views goes hand in hand with the break-through, in the *Logical Investigations*, to a proper assessment of the power and originality of Hume's theory of abstraction – an assessment which corrected Meinong's Hamiltonian misconceptions about the distinctions of reason doctrine. Then, in the second place, the unveiling of the material *a priori* by Husserl, as implicit in the theory of perception by perspective views, is closely bound up with the appearance, in the years before World War I, of a remarkable paper by Adolf Reinach, to which Husserl, in his obituary article on his pupil's death shortly afterwards at the Front, acknowledged the deepest debt for its achievement in having brought home to him the real meaning of Hume's doctrine of the relations of ideas, that is to say of necessary truths, as having a genuine affinity with the phenomenological type of material a priori developed by himself, and as having in it nothing of the analytical or tautological character attributed to Hume by Kant. Then, in the third place, some twenty years later with the final assimilation by Husserl of the import of these discoveries in the *Treatise*, and with the growing awareness on his part of the seminal role played by Hume in Western philosophy, the 1929 edition of the *Yearbook for Philosophy and Phenomenological Research* contains not only Husserl's *Formal and Transcendental Logic*, then given to the world for the first time, but also, immediately after it, the book-length article on Hume by Husserl's English postgraduate student, C. V. Salmon, a Germanified Oxonian – the two works being placed, side by side, in what I feel to be (given Husserl's editorship) a juxtaposition of a highly significant character. Here, the paradoxical dictum about 'the as yet, in its most important respect, unrecognised greatness' of *Treatise I*, contained in the *Formal and Transcendental Logic*, has its meaning highlighted and underlined by being followed

159

up immediately by the pupil's lucid and exciting demonstration that the central problem of David Hume's philosophy is constituted by the impressively profound struggle of the *Treatise* to anticipate, a century and a half before its time, the central Husserlian distinction between consciousness of object and object of consciousness, that is, *Noesis* and *Noema*, which had grown out of the doctrine of perception by perspective views.

Moreover, this underlying affinity of the central problem of the Humean philosophy with that of the Husserlian phenomenology, first discovered by Salmon under the Master's supervision in 1929, and then independently rediscovered and re-stated by another pupil Aron Gurwitsch, ten years later, is not by any means the end of the story. In a final bursting out beyond Hume but through Hume to recapture the spirit of the great philosophical movement of which Hume had been the pathfinder and pioneer in the Scotland of his time, the book on *The Crisis of the European Sciences*, which is the crown of Husserl's career, not only in effect re-stated in terms of our twentieth century the problem so much insisted on by the Scottish philosophers of the classical school as central to the whole movement of modern civilisation, that is to say the problem of the morally disruptive effects of scientific reductionism as pre-figured in the Cartesian algebra, (the problem of guarding against the danger that natural science, in the pride of its world-conquering expertise, may turn its hand against the intellectual standards to which it owed its birth); but, in addition what is just as remarkable – gave a new lease of life to the common sense critique of scientism carried through by the old Scottish school, and was indirectly to inspire, among some phenomenologists of the next generation, the project of uncovering the hidden excellence of the chef d'école of Scottish philosophy, Hume's opponent Thomas Reid, in much the same way as Husserl in his life-time had helped to uncover the hidden excellence of David Hume. Looked at in this light, Husserl's final years left behind them the legacy of a programme for a sort of phenomenological refurbishing of the philosophy of Scotland's classical age, which was, in the first place, to be excellently implemented in France by a classic article in 1954 by Professor Maxime Chastaing of the University of Dijon, a one-time pupil of J-P.Sartre, on *Thomas Reid, the Philosophy of Common Sense and the Problem of our Knowledge of Other Minds*, and also bore worthy fruit at the other side of the European Continent, in Poland, in the book on Reid – both sympathetic and stimulating as communicated to me in conversations with the author, Professor Hempelinsky then of Krackow – which, produced under the direction of Husserl's closest philosophical associate, Roman Ingarden, sanctions a sort of posthumous identification of Husserl's phenomenology with Reid to match the affinity affirmed in Husserl's lifetime of his phenomenology with the philosophy of Hume.

Thus, carried forward from its first beginnings by the wave of intellectual excitement aroused by the discussion of Hume and Hamilton in the Brentano circle, chiefly through the work of Meinong, the phenomenological movement has, in an indirect way, time after time sought fresh inspiration in a return to the ideas of Hume and the Scottish school of common sense. Whatever value and influence Husserl's central work as a creative systematic philosopher has had on the English-speaking world, there can be no doubt of the influence and value of this secondary and historically oriented work (for all that it was a throw-away spasmodic effort) in the de-sedimentation of the *Treatise* texts – in the smashing of the second-hand Hamiltonian stereotypes of Hume – which, influencing that most remarkable historian of philosophy, Norman Kemp Smith, not only provided him with the means of transforming his early articles on Naturalism in Hume into the magisterial works of his later years on *The Philosophy of David Hume* and the *Dialogues*, but also in the long run, by the spillover of Kemp Smith's infectious enthusiasm for re-assessing the intellectual inheritance of the West, prepared the way for the subsequent realization, now at long last belatedly dawning on the Scottish Universities themselves, that there was gold in the dung-hill of the common sense philosophy as accumulated in the classrooms of Scotland in the course of a full century's discussion and re-discussion of Hume's *Treatise* Book I.

Notes

1. *Letters*, ii. 452.
2. *The Wealth of Nations*, bk. v, ch. 1, pt. 3, art. 3.
3. 'Of Essay Writing' in *The Philosophical Works of David Hume* ed. T. H. Green and T. H. Grose (London 1874-5) vol. IV, pp. 367-70.

Husserl and Reinach on Hume's 'Treatise'

1 Subjectivism vs. Objectivism

In 1929 Husserl wrote that Hume's real greatness was still unrecognized in its most important aspect. I believe that the contribution to Hume studies by Husserl – as conveyed by Jean Laporte in France and Kemp Smith in Britain – and by his pupil Reinach, have gone a long way towards changing this state of affairs, because of a new way of reading Hume's Treatise that they introduced. I first set out Husserl's early views on Hume and then turn to Reinach's paper on Hume, which builds on this work, but also goes a long way beyond it and isolates the most important aspect of Hume's achievement.

I will start from the crisis which stimulated the intellectual activity of Husserl on the subject – the contrast, namely, between the subjectivist evaluation of Hume's doubts as the deepest thing in philosophy, which, consummated by Hamilton, had made a considerable impression on the German-speaking world of Husserl's youth and, as against this, the impatiently objectivist dismissal of the whole tradition of subjectivising academicism by thinkers like Gottlob Frege. Such objectivists, though sympathetic in their own way to the idea of common sense in Philosophy, were nevertheless totally out of sympathy with the paradoxical defence of it offered by Hamilton, according to which common sense is at once unshakably authoritative and yet a tissue of logical contradictions.

Hamilton agrees at the outset with the truth of the common sense view that I know how to distinguish in the sharpest possible way between the bodies I observe on the one hand and my observation of them on the other. But he goes on to insist that whenever one gets down, in a professional way, to the reflective analysis of the facts of consciousness involved in the cognitive situation, this apparently clear contrast between the body observed and my observation of it becomes extraordinarly cloudy and difficult to draw.

Hamilton calls attention to the relevance of the paradox brought up by Hume in one of those often overlooked passages towards the end of the *Treatise* chapter on the senses. An analysis of the perception of a body which seeks, in the favourite Hamiltonian phrase, to take into account 'the facts, the whole facts and nothing but the facts of consciousness' – especially the odd and illusory cases, side by side with the normal – reveals a sort of ineradicable inconsistency between one's natural belief of a naïvely realistic kind in the direct perception of a body as independent of the perceiver and one's equally natural belief in the regularity of the causal connectedness as between one aspect of the whole experience and another. The argument for common sense, Hamilton says, in a characteristic generalisation of the Humean result, 'founds on the assumption that our original beliefs are self-consistent with one another and are not self-contradictory',[1] but Hume has shown in a *de facto ad hominem* way that, as expounded by the classic philosophers, the thesis of the consistency of our natural beliefs with one another and with the facts of consciousness in general is impossible to justify. No doubt, Hamilton goes on, coming now to the second and less familiar part of the argument which is going to concern us, we can, leaving aside this particular difficulty, try as philosophers to give some foundation to the distinction between the object of perception on the one hand and the perception of the object on the other by some sort of abstractive act, somewhat similar to what happens when, with a shift of attention, we can concentrate on the coloured aspect of a coloured shape to the exclusion of the aspect of visual extension or again, concentrate on the visual extension side to the exclusion of the colour aspect. – But, while this kind of abstraction by a shift of attention does enable us to make some kind of contrast between the subjective and objective, the perceiving and the object perceived, nevertheless the distinction it draws, Hamilton goes on, is incapable of endowing the object-pole with the independence of the subject-pole which is demanded by our common sense about the external world. – No doubt the practised introspectionist finds the tightly inseparable relationships like that of ego and non-ego, or of equilaterality and equiangularity no more difficult to break down by a shift of attention than the somewhat different and looser kind of inseparability which obtains as between colour and visible shape. But the separation so effected is not the separation demanded by our belief in the independence of an external world, since in all three cases the separation is logical or mental only, and not real. In this way, Hamilton found himself finally entangled in a whole series of paradoxes which he could only defend by reference to the authoritative statement of Hume that the sharp common sense distinction between the body experienced and our experience of it, while it is impossible to draw, is also impossible to deny.

This kind of extreme subjectivism, which was very widespread at the time in Europe, and which Hamilton was notable for defending in the most provocative manner possible was to be contemptuously pushed aside by Frege in the preliminaries of his philosophy of arithmetic. No doubt Frege felt the danger to science of this intrusion into its investigations of a reflective subjectivism. If science was to achieve the desired objectivity in regard to nature, it was essential to keep our discussion of the natural qualities of the properties of bodies quite free and disentangled from our discussion of the experiences involved in getting to know these. Now there was nothing in all this, of course, with which Hamilton would disagree since he, too, in his capacity as Clerk Maxwell's chief philosophical mentor as well as in his published defence of Duncan Gregory's still important paper on *The Real Nature of Symbolical Algebra* (1838), was perfectly aware of the responsibility of science to be clearly objective. So far then the only disagreement between Hamilton and Frege is simply as to the degree of difficulty involved in the problem of separating perception from the perceived, and the real opposition between them about fundamentals only leaps to light where Frege, speaking perhaps as a sort of plain man, draws attention to the weakness of his theory of abstraction through shifts of attention which Hamilton had used to prop up his doctrine of the impossibility of ultimately distinguishing the experiencing from the experienced. Looking into himself by the intellectual introspective method of the philosophers he is criticising, Frege is unable to discover any trace of 'this wonderful faculty of not paying attention',[2] which philosophers like Hamilton had relied on so heavily in their psychologistic treatment of the problem of knowledge and perception. The psychologistic fallacy is thus due in large part – to quote Dummett – to 'the faulty theory of concept-formation due to the British Empiricists'.[3]

Husserl and Meinong on abstraction and Distinctions of Reason

It was at this point in the 1890s that Husserl was inevitably drawn into the argument because his *Philosophy of Arithmetic* had been singled out by Frege as a peculiarly appropriate target for the general attack on psychologicism and on the attentionist type of abstractionism which was used to underpin it. Acquiescing to a considerable extent in the justice of Frege's attack on the psychologism as well as on 'the faulty theory of concept-formation' associated with the British Empiricists, Husserl, nevertheless, as a man with a philosophical as well as a mathematical training, was more sensitive than Frege to the difficulties spotlighted by Hume and Hamilton. He saw how difficult it is to draw the desired distinction between on the one hand, the discussion of the subjective experiences involved in the acquisition and use of the common sense concepts of body, and, on the other hand, the objective descriptions of body which are given by scientists with the help of these same subjectively worked up concepts. In consequence, Husserl was led into a kind of a postmortem on the theory of abstraction – that is, the theory of drawing distinctions between inseparables – which, though begun in a spirit of sympathy with Frege, was soon to lead in a quite different direction. The turning point came with Husserl's realisation in the second of his *Logical Investigations*, that Hume's theory of abstraction – the distinctions of reason theory – was immensely superior, from the point of view of the problems canvassed by Frege, to the Hamiltonian theory of abstraction, not only because the Humean theory disassociated itself from the 'wonderful' faculty of inattention appealed to by Hamilton amid mockery from Frege, but also because it avoided the faulty theory of conception-formation alluded to by Dummett, according to which knowledge begins with acquaintance of purely unclassified individuals and then subsequently goes on to classify them, that is to say to form general concepts of them through noting their resemblances and differences.

No doubt there was much that was objectionable about Hume's use of the theory but that did not prevent Husserl from 'vindicating the glory' of Hume's achievement which, properly modified and corrected, might hope to illuminate profoundly the basic epistemological distinctions between universal and particular on the one hand, and appearance and reality on the other. Whatever Frege and his present-day admirers might say, these are still genuine problems for the foundations of the natural sciences. Seen in this light, Husserl's discussion of the Humean theory of abstraction was an essential moment in the breakthrough to phenomenology. Postponing his original programme of exploring the foundations of logic on lines opened out by Frege, Husserl set about re-thinking the *Treatise of Human Nature*, book I, using as his principle of investigation what one might call the de-atomised version of impressions and ideas which results from the application of the distinctions of reason technique, as this had been evolved by Hume himself.

The picture given here of the stimulating effect of the *Treatise* on Husserl's intellectual development – often overlooked by phenomenologists as well as by Hume scholars – becomes very difficult to disown as soon as one institutes a comparison between Meinong's discussion of the problem of abstraction in British Empiricism in the *Hume-Studies* of 1877[4] and Husserl's discussion of the same subject published some 25 years after Meinong in vol. 2 of *Logical Investigations* in the second Investigation 'The Ideal Unity of the Species and Modern Theories of Abstraction', in Chapter 5 of the latter under the heading 'A Phenomenological Study of Hume's Theory of Abstraction'.

Hundred-page-long treatises of comparable elaboration, both essays are concerned with precisely the same contrast between the distinctions of reason theory of abstraction as developed by Hume on the one hand, and the theory of abstraction by shifts of attention as worked up in lucid detail by Hamilton (though originally due, Meinong suggests, to Berkeley) on the other hand. And the central difference between their otherwise parallel discussions is that whereas Meinong sets aside the Humean theory of the distinctions of reason in favour of the theory of abstraction by shifts of attention as developed by Hamilton and Berkeley, in Husserl's opinion the Humean theory should be acknowledged as the really successful effort of the two. It is Hume who comes very near to solving the problem of abstraction, at least as far as the genetic aspects of the problem are concerned, whereas the Berkeley-Hamilton theory is ranked by Husserl as being inferior to Hume's and as possessing intellectual value only in so far as it asks the right question without giving the right answer. Read by itself and in isolation from Meinong, Husserl's severely critical treatment of the theories of abstraction in British Empiricism, because of all his balancing acts, might well give the impression, to the unwary reader, that he is no more sympathetic to Hume's theory than to the other theory; but read in comparison with Meinong, Husserl's growing identification with Hume stands out with unmistakable clarity.

Let us get down to our problem by contrasting these two remarkable German-language discussions of English-language philosophy. An exegetical study which mingles in a most lively way the history of ideas with their philosophical assessment, Meinong's *Hume Studies I* aims to defend the Berkeley-Hamilton theory of abstraction by shifts of attention by destroying Hume's attempt to produce an alleged case of the experience of a body in which attention could not possibly distinguish between its inseparable aspects of shape and colour. The climax of Meinong's argument consists in his trying to convict Hume of an infinite regress. Hume had advanced the startling claim that, if a globe of white marble is contemplated in relation to an adjacent globe of black marble and a cube of white, we can become aware of the first object as being of a dual character and so can be in a position to attend alternately to the colour aspect and the shape aspect, in virtue of our recognising it as resembling the one object in the one way and the other in another. But Hume argues, if we consider the white globe of marble by itself, putting out of court the resemblance relationships which provide us with our evidence of its duality, we lose the evidence for differentiating between the shape and the colour and so lose the ability to attend to either. The point thus made, Meinong says, is no doubt, highly ingenious, but it is no good at all as an argument. Hume has failed to see that if it is impossible for our vision to shift the attention as between the shape and the colour when we are confronted with them in a single object because the colour and the shape are given simultaneously and inseparably to sight, it is, by the same token, equally impossible for our vision, when faced by the three objects in a row, to shift its attention from the shape relations to the colour relations because the shape relations and the colour relations of the three bodies as given to our vision, possess the same sort of simultaneity and inseparability as was possessed by the colour aspect and the shape aspect in the single object. Hume's solution of the problem, according to Meinong, has ended in a vicious regress.[5]

When, twenty-five years later, Husserl discusses the same passages in Hume, he is also concerned with the possibility of a vicious regress, but, in contrast to Meinong, he proceeds in a much more discriminating manner. The conditions in which Hume's analysis of the white globe case might be cleared of these implications of a vicious regress are made plain by Husserl in the light of a comparison with a contrasting set of conditions in which an incorrect development of Hume does indeed lead to an infinite regress.

The danger of the vicious regress, Husserl insists, lies in a reductionist interpretation of the distinctions of reason theory. Taking up Hume's theory, German empiricists like Cornelius, says Husserl (*Logical Investigations*, vol. I, Investigation II, §39 and Appendix 6), draw the consequence that the distinction between shape and colour is a mere fiction and that there is neither colour in the coloured thing nor shape in the shaped thing, our perception of the distinction between the two being nothing but the perception of the various resemblance relationships in which the thing considered is involved.[6] But this way of developing Hume, Husserl points out, at once leads to the contradiction complained of by Meinong, since if a philosopher wished 'to maintain that when we think we perceive, e.g. the property of white, we really only perceive, or otherwise present to ourselves, a resemblance between the apparent object and other objects,' then such a man 'has involved himself in an infinite regress since talk of this presented resemblance calls for a corresponding re-interpretation.' (*ibid.* § 37, 41).

But as against all this, the distinctions of reason theory, Husserl proceeds, can be freed from the fatally reductive implications pointed out by Meinong if it is re-stated in terms of a more sophisticated theory of perception than Hume's, according to which the globe of white marble, even when considered alone and without reference to the black globe and the white cube, does not present itself as a simple undifferentiated object but, even in this relatively isolated state, shows itself to possess a highly complicated range of distinctive properties, already inclusive of the very distinction denied by Hume himself, namely that

172

of colour and shape. According to Husserl, for the natural attitude, or common sense, the marble globe offers itself as simultaneously and inseparably white and spherical with a constant colour and a constant shape. But reflective analysis, which digs beneath common sense, reveals a whole series of semi-conscious differentiations and identifications missed alike by Meinong (*ibid.* §§ 32–33; Note 2 to § 37) and by Hume himself. In these the perceiver finds himself engaged by turns in the analogous but contrasting, and to some extent alternating, process of discounting (i) changes in the globe's illumination – e.g.. from white to grey – as due, not to any change on the part of the globe itself, but to the overshadowing effect of his own bodily movements as perceiver; (ii) the changes in the appearances presented by the globe – e.g. from round to oval – as caused not by a real shape-alteration in it but once again by his own change from a full frontal gaze to a sidelong glance.

'On the one hand, we are concerned with the *sphere itself* and its inner properties, e.g. its uniform white colouring: on the other hand we are concerned with the *appearance of the sphere* and the complex of sensations immanent in it, among which is, e.g. the continuously graded *abschattende* sensation of white – the subjective correlate of the objective white which is uniformly apparent in perception. Here as elsewhere, Hume left this difference quite unnoticed; for him appearance and the apparent phenomenon coalesce. (*ibid.* § 36, 409).'

It is because Hume does not go the full length of this reflective analysis but remains in the naïve and natural attitude here that he comes to view the colour and shape of the solitary globe as presenting themselves as undifferentiated or as one and the same.

Husserl now goes on to restore the balance. Hume, he insists, is not wholly wrong in his analysis since the colour-shape difference as originarily presented by the solitary object, by way of the afore-mentioned perceptual *Abschattungen*, is a rudimentary difference which exhibits the contrasting aspects as still tightly bound up in a sort of interdependence, and conceals their separateness. The aspect-difference thus revealed is emphatically characterised by Husserl (§§ 38, 39 especially 418 top) as 'vague but clear', 'rough but self-evident' in much the same way as a uniformly and unbrokenly white expanse as perceived originarily, is divided up into spatial demarcations only in the light of the ever-present but normally neglected experience of the illusive shifting boundaries which briefly and fleetingly make their appearance and disappear again, as the result of the afforementioned perceptual shadings (*Abschattungen*). Such demarcations have about them nothing of the objective definiteness of division brought into being in the unbroken white expanse when lines are drawn across it or when for some reason half of it turns red, the rest remaining white (§ 39, 418–9). Hume himself no doubt takes no notice whatever of the vague spatiality already contained in the first experience of the unbroken white expanse or – to take his own example – an encircling gloom, describing this latter as 'without parts, without composition, invariable and indivisible' (*Treatise*, 57)[7] therefore non-spatial just as in the corresponding passage on the globe of white marble, he treats the colour and the shape as originarily one and indistinguishable

174

and takes no notice of the rudimentary type of distinction, spotlighted by Husserl, which begins to prise the two aspects apart without however effecting a proper separation. But, at the same time, Husserl's listing of these oversights by Hume has the effect of bringing out by contrast that part of the problem which Hume really had grasped. What Hume has illuminated is the traditionally very difficult point as to how we can talk about a thing's colour without talking about its visible shape or vice-versa though the two are always given together in a sort of interdependence, or how we can talk meaningfully of the encircling gloom, or the blue of the sky (*Treatise* 56) as if they were measurable objects capable of definite demarcation like the star-spangled night sky when, empirically speaking or considered in themselves, – prior to the appearance of the stars – they have no such properties. To have discovered all this is no mean achievement on Hume's part, Husserl makes clear, even though in deference to the enemies of philosophical analysis we have to call it psychology.

Regarded from Husserl's standpoint, Meinong's criticisms of Hume's distinctions of reason as involving a regress would seem, then, to miss the mark completely. Consider, first, the vital question whether as Meinong alleges, Hume was wrong in claiming that whereas it is impossible to distinguish by shifts of attention between the colour and shape of a white globe when it is presented in isolation, it becomes possible to switch the attention from the one to the other when, instead of a solitary object, we see the object compared and flanked with the other two objects. Husserl's answer would seem to be that Hume is plainly right if one takes into account, what Hume's language surely implies, but what Meinong failed to note, that when we have the three objects before us we can look at them in different ways, taking in all three in our gaze, or concentrating on two and leaving the other in the background etc. in a way which cannot happen when the one object is presented to us by itself. That is to say, from Husserl's point of view, the case of the three objects permits, in addition to the comparisons, a shift of perspectives which makes the separation possible as between the two inseparable aspects.

In the second place, if in order to justify Hume against Meinong, it is permitted to take into account the eye movements etc. in addition to the comparisons then surely we are also entitled to take them into account when we contemplate the globe of white marble by itself, thus making possible the shifts of perspective view which enable us to distinguish in a rudimentary way within the solitary object a colour aspect as well as a shape aspect in a way that Hume did not suspect. In this way the critical re-working over of Meinong's refutation of Hume, not only re-instates Hume against Meinong but prepares the way for Husserl's famous *Abschattungen*.

In all this, Husserl, without perhaps realising what he was doing, is clearly getting far away from Frege and is beginning to reach out towards a re-discovered and renovated Hume, not the old subjectivist Hume of Hamilton's article on Brown,[8] but the Hume buried in the unread pages of the *Treatise*, which had never seen the light of day since the book had fallen dead-born from the press. At the same time, however, Husserl's re-discovery of Hume is still impeded by the anxiety, not to say irritation, communicated from Frege about the sceptical implications of the Humean approach. These over-sophisticated speculations of Hume about an experience which entirely confounds the essential distinction between shape and colour – are they not a gratuitous attack on common sense which, if pushed too far, would make objective science impossible? In his anxiety to keep at bay the scepticism which will perversely identify shape and colour, Husserl takes refuge in the great fact of common sense which, according to him, Humean scepticism wantonly controverts – namely, that 'we deceive ourselves' only about details i.e. only 'when we leave the sphere of gross differences'. 'Just as the difference between a cockchafer and a pine-tree ... has genuine self-evidence', so we believe with a genuine self-evidence, likewise, in a colour-moment as being 'really *there* in our unitary intuition helping to build up the latter and quite different from the moment of shape that is likewise present'. (LI 413). No doubt, the colour and the shape, Husserl goes on, are bound up with one another in some sort of inseparable relation, but it is nonsense to suggest, as Hume seems to do, that because of the fact of their inseparability the colour and shape are more liable than the pine-tree and the cockchafer to be confused together in a false identification. As if proud of this earthy example of the cockchafer and the pine-tree, Husserl employs it in a heavy-handed manner no less than three times with the same object in view as Professor Austin had, according to Ved Mehta, in the more light-hearted example of the cocktail glass and the swizzle-stick – to silence the misplaced scepticism of the Humeans and to restore Fregean good sense.

In all this, however, Husserl has not yet established the closer rapport with Hume which was later to develop, and, in his critique of this so-called scepticism seems to me to go very far astray. The fact of the matter is – I believe – that, in speaking of the possibility of failing to differentiate the colour and shape of a thing Hume was not on a sceptical tack at all, but was raising a too often neglected and quite real question which has worried other Scottish philosophers – notably Hamilton (1853, 695–6) in his controversy with de Morgan – the question, namely, as to what is meant by saying 'the colour is distinct from the shape' or, for that matter, 'the cockchafer is different from the pine-tree'. What Hume is driving at is simply that if one knows what one means when one pronounces A to be distinct from B one must also by the same token be able to make sense, in an empirical kind of way, of the counter assertion that A is not different from B. That is to say, the understanding of what is meant by the denial and the assertion of the same distinction is not merely a verbal matter, and one must be able to specify the empirical conditions in which the distinction appears in contrast to the empirical conditions in which it fails to materialise. When therefore *Treatise I* (34, line 14) cites an out-of-the way experience in which the colour-shape distinction seems impossible to make – in his very first visual experience a blind man who can suddenly see catches a glimpse of a bright yellow moon suddenly appearing out of a previously quite dark sky, without having the memory or experience of any other visual object to compare it with – Hume is not concerned to shake our confidence in the power of our knowledge, but simply to make the same sort of point

178

as Georges van Riet, (in a circulated type-script of the lecture which supplied materials for his article on the Thomistic Theory of Abstraction) perhaps had in mind when he says that if every brazen object were spherical and every spherical object were brazen the difference between the two would not materialise in language. Hume's point is thus that the distinction in question is not merely a matter of verbal convention but depends on experience and he goes to great lengths to bring this out by exhibiting other peculiar cases – as for example, the odd case, mentioned in *Treatise* Bk I, Part 2, Section III (34) of our having as our original objects of vision nothing but purple shapes, shining no doubt out of the dark and indistinguishable background of nothingness discussed in Section V, but 'afterwards having experience of the other colours of violet, green, red, white, black'. The object of such examples is, apparently, to suggest that in spite of the inseparability of colour and visual shape, there could be languages where there were colour-words but no shape-words, or shape-words with no colour-words, e.g. in which the shape (called by Hume 'the composition of colour points') was constant and the colour varied, or in which the colour (e.g. purple) was constant and the shape varied. Moreover, it does not make any difference to the principle at stake whether we are dealing with inseparables like colour and shape or separables like Husserl's cockchafer and pine-tree or the proverbial chalk and cheese, since the analogous principle applies in these latter cases too in the sense that a distinction of the cockchafer as a body independent of the pine-tree could hardly be in evidence if the world was so arranged that every such tree had that kind of beetle perched on its top and there wasn't any beetle of that sort found anywhere else. Far from mischieviously seeking to undermine common sense or pervert our understanding of the distinctions of ordinary language, Hume is simply engaging in the philosopher's work of the analysis of the familiar – an analysis which, as he points out in Section I of the *Principles of the Human Understanding* (last five paragraphs) cannot be carried through without making the familiar look very unfamiliar, that is to say, without warping ordinary language.

In making these claims for Hume, I do not mean to imply that, in the last analysis, Husserl goes entirely astray. On the contrary, the objection to be brought against him is that his treatment of Hume is unilluminating not in the sense of giving an unjustifiable interpretation, but rather in the sense of giving an ambiguous one. On the one hand, Husserl is engaged in pointing out that the element of an extreme and indefensible scepticism first makes its appearance in the *Treatise* in the passage where Hume is speaking of the empirical foundations of the spatial demarcations attributed by common sense to the experience of the blue[9] of the sky or the dark indistinguishability of night, whereas in the discussion in the *Treatise* of the separation of shape from colour, the analytic procedures of the distinctions of reason are used in a moderate manner which is philosophically fruitful. But on the other hand, in the midst of all this, Husserl is also quite consciously propounding the alternative suggestion that the radical kind of scepticism which vitiates the discussion of how we demarcate the night sky is already present in the discussion of the colour-shape case, and confounds a distinction which ought to be as plain as that of the cockchafer and the pine-tree. Thus, Husserl starts perceptively from a position which sees the root-problem of the *Treatise* as arising out of the difficulty of tracing the relationship between the developed experience in which this or that distinction between inseparables – e.g. particular and general, or appearance and reality – manifests itself, on the one hand, and the contrasting simplified experience in which the same distinction disappears from view, on the other hand. Husserl then proceeds to oscillate between a favourable interpretation and an unfavourable interpretation of Hume's analytic method. On the favourable view, the *Treatise* begins successfully enough by exhibiting the colour-shape separation as a fiction *cum fundamento in re*, i.e. as a fiction having some genuine foundation in reality, and only gets entangled in confusion and contradiction when the Humean analysis represents the spatial partition of the dark indistinguishability of the night as being a fiction *sine fundamento in re*, i.e. as a kind of association-manufactured illusion. But alternating with this lenient judgment, a correspondingly unfavourable view of Hume's procedures makes itself heard according to which the search for the empirical basis of these distinctions without a separation, because of its being uncritically used, gets the *Treatise* entangled from the very start in the kind of vicious regress spoken of by Meinong even in the case of the colour-shape distinction. Thus, the difficulty with the *Logical Investigations* here is that Husserl finds himself in two minds as to whether or not the method of analysis deployed by Hume in *Treatise I* – the distinctions of reason method

– is or is not a legitimate and fruitful procedure in philosophy, and in the event, this prince of modern rationality, otherwise so note-worthy for the unvarying serenity of his intellectual self-confidence, is obliged – like many another – to confess himself as being in a quandary over Hume's intentions. 'I am not really sure,' Husserl finally admits, 'whether I have hit off Hume's own view' (LI 409–10) because of the difficulty of knowing what he means by calling the globe of white marble a simple object. If he means by this that the contrasting characters already exist in the object in an inseparable unity prior to the comparison and that the function of the comparison is simply to make them *thinkable* independently of one another, then plainly his problem has a good sense, but if what he means is that prior to the comparison the contrasting characters have no existence whatever in the object, and that the comparison has the function of bringing them into being, then his problem is a spurious one. After all his meticulous examination of the texts, Husserl is unable to decide whether Hume is carrying on, where Berkeley left off, the valuable work of re-discovering the reality of the old relation of distinguishability between what is inseparable against that of mere separability, or whether the object of the *Treatise* discussion is simply to eliminate altogether the scholastic *abstractio* by reducing it to a *separatio* (LI 410, 411).

3 Reinach on Hume and 'a priori' Truths

So far, what Husserl chiefly values the distinctions of reason passage for is that, unintentionally or otherwise, Hume's discovery (or rather, re-discovery – following Berkeley), there and elsewhere, of propositions of the 'synthetic a priori' type like *colour involves extension*, shows up very clearly the shortcomings of the normal doctrine of British empiricists from J. S. Mill onward, to the effect that there are only two types of proposition – the purely analytic or verbal sort like *bachelors = unmarried men*, and the purely synthetic sort like *no smoke without fire*. And yet, along with this reluctant admiration, Husserl continued to be severely critical of the Humean philosophy for its failure to allow a place for the more difficult and recondite distinctions of reason which had been the object of 'metaphysical abstraction' in the Scholastic times – e.g. the relation of distinguishability but inseparability as holding between the apparent and the real, or, what more immediately concerns us, between the general and the particular. Far from using the distinctions of reason technique to vindicate the complicated position of the general as at once independent of the particular, and yet interdependent with it, the Humean philosophy, as Husserl understood it, had the consciously anti-metaphysical aim of seeking to eliminate the former item in the contrast – viz. the general – by reducing it to the particular, conceived in an atomistic manner.

Adolf Reinach's very remarkable article on *Kant's understanding of the Humean Problem*[10] or, as it might be more fitly titled, *Kant's Misunderstanding of the Humean Problem* showed clearly that Hume's doctrine of the Universal was not reductive. Hume, according to Reinach, was not merely a philosopher of the empiricist party who was committed on his official self-conscious position to its idea of the tautology as the only kind of *a priori*, and whose chief merit consisted in a blind groping towards a different and more complex kind of non-tautologistic necessity, implicit in the discussion of colour and shape, without really knowing what exactly he was doing and without in the least coming near Kant's profound insights into the necessary proposition as an *a priori* synthesis. Digging deep into that extra-ordinary section on Knowledge which serves as the introduction to Part 3 of *Treatise I*, Adolf Reinach in an article which to the German quality of thoroughness adds a crispness, clarity and wit unexpected in German philosophy, confounded the stereotyped views of the *Treatise* by pointing out that far from groping unconsciously towards a more adequate idea of necessary truth and universality, Hume had already consciously reached this goal. Far from requiring to be patronised for having tentatively prepared the way for Kant's more solid achievement in reference to necessary and general truth, he had already out-distanced Kant, at any rate in respect of explaining a very fundamental part of the field of necessary truth which Kant himself had left unvisited. The first point Reinach makes is the indefensibility of the Kantian claim, still too widely accepted, that Hume misses the synthetic character of the necessary truths of mathematics through an oversight, and holds them to be simply analytic. Kant's view of the matter, Reinach goes on, is completely at variance with the plainly enunciated doctrine of *Treatise* I, Book 3, Section I, which draws a highly original and far reaching distinction between necessary propositions and contingent propositions. Hume here shows

184

that in the case of contingent propositions relations can vary without variation in the related objects – as occurs in a change of place relations where a billiard ball, on being pushed to the other end of the table is not altered in its general character by the movements which destroy its side-by-side relations with another billiard ball. But, Hume goes on, necessary propositions deal with relations which cannot change except in virtue of a change in the character of the related objects. Thus, in a right-angled triangle, the relation of equality between the square on the hypotenuse and the sum of the squares on the other two sides is such that it cannot be changed without a change in the character of the related objects, – as, by changing the right angle into an obtuse angle, one brings it about that the sum of the squares on the two unchanged sides is less than the square on the now longer hypotenuse. Can it be objected that this example of the hypotenuse case gets Hume away from the idea that a geometrical proposition is analytic, only at the price of representing it to be a contingent proposition in the ordinary sense? But Adolf Reinach deals with this objection by pointing to a salient, too little noticed, fact about this passage in the *Treatise*. Namely, that as instances of the peculiar sort of proposition under consideration, in which the 'relation is invariable as long as our idea [of the objects] remains the same' (*Treatise* Book I, Part 3, Section I, 9, 70), Hume includes not only geometrical and arithmetical propositions, but also propositions about the resemblance relations of qualities, such as *red is like orange*, which are not contingent in the ordinary sense. Thus, just as the relation between the square on the hypotenuse and the sum of the squares on the other two sides alters if one changes the right angle into an acute or obtuse angle, the same is true of two analogous examples in another sphere, Reinach's *red resembles orange* and Hume's *blue resembles green*. The latter relationship, cited by Hume in an important footnote[11] is explained by him as meaning that blue and green resemble one another by comparison with scarlet. The relation, that is, alters as soon as one changes the objects or ideas under consideration to the extent of substituting for the scarlet a blueygreen mid-shade, for the result of this is that the blue and green instead of resembling one another become different or unlike, considered in relation to the midshade. But then it becomes impossible to claim that Hume has got away from the view that geometrical propositions are analytic by treating them as contingent propositions in the sense of being propositions about the external relations of objects, for the case of the relationship between the green and the blue and the scarlet shows quite clearly that the class of relationships intended when Hume speaks of the relations as remaining invariable so long as the ideas remain the same are not external relations at all – as in the case of the billiard balls that do not change their quality in changing their position – but internal relations. An example of an internal relation cited by Hume in the same important appendix-addition is the fact that 'particular sounds ... admit of infinite resemblances upon general appearance and comparison',[12] i.e. that, as I understand it, a given sound will sound somewhat different according to the different sounds it is heard along with.

Reinach has found in this passage in the *Treatise*

upon the internal relatedness of colour qualities a doctrine, which, consciously entertained by Hume, approximates to the phenomenologist's favourite example of a material *a priori* principle that *colour involves physical extension*. Opening up the hidden places in the *Treatise*, Reinach shows that Hume has already anticipated the doctrine of the *Logical Investigations,* not merely with the non-tautological tie-up of colour and extension, not merely with the internal relatedness of red, yellow and orange but also in the passage on the missing shade of blue.[13] For in this passage Hume had already adumbrated the characteristically Husserlian claim that even if, by some technical expertise, all of the colour orange had been blotted out of the world so that none was visible it would still remain true that orange is midway between red and yellow.

In the Obituary article written by Husserl on Reinach's death in World War I, the first and principal item is a warm personal acknowledgement of the great value of what he has to say on 'Kant's grasp of the Humean Problem'.[14] Husserl himself, as we now know, had in fact anticipated Reinach's criticism of Kant. In a text that was probably written no later than 1903 Husserl had pointed out that in the *Treatise* Hume denies that mathematics consists of tautologies.[15]

For Hume as for Husserl, the contingency and surprise of which the world was full, was itself limited by necessity, at least in the sense that the shape and colour of things, though themselves ascertainable only *a posteriori* in their changes, must nevertheless in all their variations conform to certain fixed laws of shape relation and colour relation. These laws are discoverable *a priori* by an intuition made possible by a reflective analysis on experience of just the type pioneered in the Humean distinctions of reason. Thus for the observation of the world on which science depends, the colour and shape of things involved with one another in the inseparable necessity of an interdependence nevertheless allows, up to a point, the colour variations to be relatively independent of the shape variations and vice versa. But in addition, just as the shape variations in three dimensions – to take the familiar case – have to operate under conditions of internal relatedness which geometry seeks to unfold *a priori*, so too, in a somewhat analogous way colour changes have to take place within the fixed laws of an internal relatedness such as the position of orange between red and yellow. Thus it is true that what is to happen to the shape of a baby's head in later life or to the colour of its complexion is a contingent fact to be ascertained only by recording and preserving observations. But as Hume has already realised, or come near to realising and as Husserl points out at the very beginning of *Ideas* I, the question as to whether the baby's head is to remain round or become oval or whether its complexion is to be ruddy or pale or sallow can only be intelligibly canvassed provided the laws regulating the relations of the shape qualities or again of the colour qualities are themselves not contingent and still less conventional, but fixedly rooted in the nature of things. Yielding up its secrets to Adolf Reinach's inspired interpretation, *Treatise* I reveals itself as containing in its hidden depths a vein of phenomenological analysis which has two great merits. Not only does it vindicate, in the face of a one-sided empiricism, a place for universality and necessity. Within the sphere of the universal and the necessary, the *Treatise* also establishes, as against a monistic reductivism like Bradley's, the rights of the 'abstract' perspective on relations like shape and colour. These are, in a certain way, independent and extensional. Yet though the rights of the 'concrete' perspective on the same relations as being, in a certain way, internal and intentional, are also defended, the former are not depreciated in comparison with the latter in the favourite Hegelian fashion.

Reinach's stimulating but tantalisingly incomplete exhibition of the range and novelty of the whole Humean treatment of *a priori* as applying to mathematics and causal necessity over and above regional necessity had the effect of awakening a new curiosity and even hope that more pertinacious research might disclose in *Treatise* I other intellectual riches, equally relevant to the phenomenological programme.

4 Salmon and Kemp Smith on Abstraction

In 1929 Husserl printed the doctoral thesis of his Oxonian pupil C.V. Salmon[16] in his *Jahrbuch* side by side with *Formale und Transcendentale Logik*. Salmon entirely breaks with the view – still common among phenomenologists – that Hume's notion of analysis in *Treatise* I is atomistic. On the contrary, as Salmon argues in this thesis that was so highly praised by Husserl, there is nothing wrong with Hume's method of analysis, which in fact, is not atomistic, but abstractive in somewhat the same sense as Husserl's.

What makes the *Treatise* analysis go astray, and end in scepticism about the external world, is simply Hume's failure to stick consistently to the abstractive method which he had discovered in an inspired moment of philosophical genius. Properly understood, Hume's theory of abstraction, Salmon says, is a remarkable bit of philosophy in the sense of its opening up a fruitful field of phenomenology which Husserl was later to explore in detail. Illustrating by a textual study more careful than any other I know, the numerous passages in the *Treatise* which show Hume on the point of breaking through to the Husserlian distinctions of noesis/noema, protention/retention Salmon argues very convincingly that Hume ultimately missed phenomenology only because he was not resolute enough in consistently carrying through the inward turn of subjectivisation.

Published in Germany in 1929, in the conscious hope – as Professor Wm. Kneale remembers[17] – of introducing the English-speaking world to phenomenology, Salmon's 'Central Problem of David Hume's Philosophy' did not, in the event, do anything for Husserl's reputation in Britain or America, but, instead, was to exercise a decisive stimulus on Hume studies, on account of Norman Kemp Smith's admiration of it. Not only was Kemp Smith's review in *Mind* (1930) the place where the importance of Hume's theory of abstraction – the distinction of reasons theory – was first brought to the notice of the English speaking world in the present century, but it is plain enough from Kemp Smith's acknowledgements in the preface and from the detailed discussion of his text that the main inspiration of his *The Philosophy of*

David Hume is the cross-fertilisation between his own 1905 commonsense interpretation of the *Treatise* on the one hand, and the phenomenological vein in Hume's theory of abstraction as revealed not only by Salmon, but also by Meinong's *Hume-Studies*, and Mrs Maund's Meinongian book on Hume,[18] to all of which Kemp Smith confesses indebtedness.

In my opinion, the most valuable contribution of Kemp Smith is that his powerful mind, using the phenomenologists' insights into Hume, succeeds in taking up from where the phenomenologists left off the problem of disentangling what is fruitful from what is false in the theory of abstraction which constitutes Hume's starting-point.

'Though Hume has here (in discussing abstraction) gone back on his principle that only the separable is distinguishable, he has not gone back – so far as the example here is concerned – upon his other principles that every perception is absolutely determinate. What he is allowing, therefore, is that within the absolutely determinate distinctions can be drawn; and so he in effect undercuts all reason for denying the distinction between the determinate and the determinable. In this way the example he uses (the 'globe of white marble') obscures the real extent of the admissions made, and conceals from him the inconsistences and insufficiencies of his argument.'[19]

Of the two points made by Kemp Smith, the one about determinability is much more important, from the standpoint of this paper, than that about separability. When Norman Kemp Smith makes the point that Hume does not give up his thesis that all impressions or perceptions are determinate, the value of this observation is that it clarifies and reinforces the sound part of the criticisms of Hume made by Husserl in the *Logical Investigation*. Starting from the remarkable insight that the knowledge of new qualities in perception arises from out of the way comparisons like that in which Newton saw the falling apple as a kind of moon, David Hume, according to Kemp Smith and Husserl, goes astray when, in trying to explain this fact of discovery by comparison, he sees the role of comparisons not as making explicit or perceptible qualities of a body which, previous to the comparisons, were implicit and imperceptible but rather as creating by association a new and additional quality which was not there before. Prior to the comparison with the globe of black marble and the cube of white, the shape and colour of the original object, the globe of white marble, was one and indistinguishable but the result of these comparisons enables us to do what we could not do before – classify this globe of white marble in two different ways – with respect to shape and colour. So far Hume, for Norman Kemp Smith and Husserl, is very profound and the weakness sets in with his associationistic explanations of the transition from an awareness of the object as undifferentiated to an awareness of it as differentiated. Instead of speaking of qualities added by association, Hume should have accepted the idea of hidden qualities, at present unobservable but waiting to be discovered. No doubt, this idea might have seemed difficult for Hume to adapt to his empiricism, but the disadvantage of the associationistic line he chooses instead is that it leads to his view of the associatively produced qualities as fictitious and, in that way, gives rise to the scepticism of Book I.

The especial value of Kemp Smith's point in connexion with Husserl's insights is that it does not relate just to the one case of the globe of white marble discussed in connection with the problem of the relation of the general to the individual, but applies to Hume's treatment of all the main distinctions of *Treatise* I between bodies as filling space and empty space, between causality and casuality between a body as it exists in my experience, and a body as it exists for itself, outside experience, not to mention the distinction over which Hume consciously admitted defeat – the distinction between objects of consciousness, impressions and ideas, on the one hand, and the self or continuing subject to which they are referred on the other.

So much for Kemp Smith on the determinable/determinate distinction. Kemp Smith's other assertion is that in his discussion of the globe of white marble Hume has given up this principle that what is distinguishable is separable or separately given. Here, I am afraid, I must demur. Hume, as I see him, never gives up this principle, and the point Norman Kemp Smith was making ought rather to be restated. First, in the globe of white marble case and various other parallel cases – the distinction between the length and breadth of a highway, or the various qualities inherent in a sound, such as pitch, timbre and loudness – Hume by the process of double comparisons, gives a very 'tolerable'[20] elucidation of how experience can make possible the shifts of attention which here enable us to separate the distinguishable aspects which, in the ob-

193

ject considered in isolation, are inseparable. But secondly, in a great many other more complicated cases, notably those which arise about personal identity and immateriality of the soul, where his scheme self-confessedly breaks down, Hume finds it is impossible in principle to discover the empirical comparisons his method of distinctions of reason requires.

I should however add – speaking now myself – that the shipwreck of the voyage taken in Book I does not mean the shipwreck of the *Treatise* as a whole. In Books II and III of the *Treatise*, Hume returns to this problem of separating the inseparable. The distinctions of reason which elude his Cartesian solitary search into the nature of mind and self in Book I suddenly came into view when, in Books II and III, he approaches the problem of self-knowledge from the standpoint of social experience and of inter-subjectivity. Here too Hume's argument is full of confusion, but this time it is not, as in the latter part of Book I, barren, but fruitful. The result is an approach to the problem of self-knowledge in conscience and in social ethics which is not only carried further by Hume himself in the two *Enquiries* and in the *Dissertation on the Passions* where he consciously but silently corrects some of his *Treatise* confusions, but which provides a starting point for Adam Smith's social philosophy and Thomas Reid's philosophy of common sense. To pursue this further would however require another discussion dealing with a third article which has made the same unforgettable impression on me as Reinach's and Salmon's – viz. Maxime Chastaing's 'Thomas Reid. La philosophie du sens commun et le problème de la connaissance d'autrui'.[21]

Postscript (1985)

Written for the 1976 Hume congress at Edinburgh, but withheld from publication the present paper has gained considerably in value in the interval, because of the unexpected complementing and corroboration of its thesis in 1980 with the appearance of Richard T. Murphy's *Hume and Husserl: towards radical subjectivism* (The Hague: Nijhoff). Both of us tell in our different ways the story as to how the inward turn in which Husserl, under Cartesian influence, set aside his earlier objectivism ultimately led him beyond Descartes to David Hume. Central to Murphy's work as to mine is the claim that the apparent change in Husserl's position was due in large part to his going back to the critique of Hume's Theory of Abstraction which was formulated at the beginning of the century in the second of the *Logical Investigations*. Finally, what is very remarkable in understanding and assessing the part of Hume which was vital for Husserl, Murphy, like myself, was greatly helped by the sections on the distinction of reason in *The Philosophy of David Hume* (263–270) by my teacher Norman Kemp Smith.

Coinciding with me as regards his general line, Murphy differs in the sense that, severely analytical, his chief concern is to show the role of Husserl's reversion to the *Logical Investigations* discussion of Hume in the move from the 'descriptive' phenomenology of the earlier period to the 'genetic' phenomenology of the final period.

Notes

1. Sir William Hamilton *Discussions on Philosophy and Literature,* second edition, 1853, 90.
2. G. Frege Posthumous Writings, translated by P. Long and R. White, Oxford 1975, 70-71; quoted by Michael Dummett *Frege – Philosophy of Language,* London: Duckworth, 1973, 158.
3 Dummett ibid., xxiv.
4 A Meinong 'Hume-Studien I. Zur Geschichte und Kritik des modernen Nominalismus' (first publication 1877), in A. Meinong's *Gesamtausgabe* Graz: Akademische Druck- u. Verlagsanstalt, Band I (1969), 1-72. 'Hume-Studien II. Zur Relationstheorie' (first publication 1882), in A. Meinong's *Gesamtausgabe,* Band II, (1971), 1-172. English translation in Kenneth Barber *Meinong's Hume Studies: Translation and Commentary,* 1966. This contains: 'Hume Studies I. On the history and criticism of modern nominalism', 98-192, which is a complete translation of Meinong 1877; 'Hume Studies II. The Theory of Relations', which is an incomplete translation of Meinong 1882.
5. Meinong 1969, 60.
6. E. Husserl *Logical Investigations,* (= LI) Vols. I and II, translated by J. N. Findlay, London: Routledge, 1970. Page references are to Vol. I of this edition.
7. David Hume *A Treatise of Human Nature,* edited by L. A. Selby-Bigge, revised by P. H. Nidditch, Oxford, 1978, Book I, Part 5, Section V. Page references are to this edition.
8. Sir W. Hamilton 'The Philosophy of Perception' in Hamilton 1853, 86-99.
9. Hume *Treatise,* Book I, Part 2, Section V, 56, lines 27-35.
10. A Reinach 'Kants Auffassung des Humeschen Problems' in *Zeitschrift für Philosophie und philosopische Kritik,* 141, 1911, 176-209. Also in GS, 1-35. English translation by J. N. Mohanty, 'Kant's Interpretation of Hume's Problem' in *Southwestern Journal of Philosophy,* 7, 1976, 161-188.
11. Footnote to *Treatise* Book I, Part 1, Section VII, 20, which is contained in the Appendix to the *Treatise,* 637.
12. *ibidem.*
13. *Treatise,* Book I, Part 3, Section I, 69, 70.
14. E. Husserl 'Adolf Reinach', in *Kant-Studien,* 23, 1919, 147-149.
15. E. Husserl *Erste Philosophie,* Husserliana VII, 1956 352.
16. In a conversation with Professor Kneale who had spoken with Husserl about the 'hochbegabte Salmon'.
17. C. V. Salmon 'The Central Problem of David Hume's Philosophy – an Essay towards a Phenomenological Interpretation of the First Book of the Treatise of Human Nature' in *Jahrbuch für Philosophie und phänomenologische Forschung,* Vol. X, 1929, 299-449.
18. Maund, Hume's *Theory of Knowledge,* London, 1932.
19. N. Kemp-Smith *The Philosophy of David Hume* London 1941, 266.
20. Salmon 1929, 334.
21. Revue Philosophique, 79, 1954, 352-399.